CANYON COUNTRY
PREHISTORIC INDIANS

THEIR CULTURES, RUINS, ARTIFACTS AND ROCK ART

by
F.A. Barnes
and
Michaelene Pendleton

An illustrated guide to understanding
the prehistoric Indian cultures
of the general Four Corners region,
with sections listing sites
where the remnants of these cultures
can be viewed.

ANOTHER
CANYON COUNTRY
GUIDE BOOK

1995
Wasatch Publishers

This book is the THIRTEENTH in a series of practical guides to travel and recreation in the scenic Colorado Plateau region of the Four Corners states.

The chapter on prehistoric Indian cultures was written by Michaelene Pendleton. All other written material, charts, and photographs are by F.A. Barnes unless otherwise credited.

Revised Seventh Printing 1995

Artwork
by
Michaelene Pendleton

Museum reconstruction of occupied Anasazi dwellings at Chaco Canyon National Monument, New Mexico.

Copyright © 1979, 1995
Wasatch Publishers
4460 Ashford Drive
Salt Lake City, UT 84124
All rights reserved
ISBN 0-915272-24-5
LCN 79-65599

CONTENTS

Betatakin ruins, Navajo National Monument, Arizona.

FOREWORD

The purpose of this guide book is to provide a summary of what is presently known about the cultures of the prehistoric American Indians who once occupied the vast Four Corners region, and to help canyon country visitors find and appreciate some of the tangible remnants of these cultures.

To do this, we have combined the efforts of two authors into one book, with one author describing the prehistoric Indians as they lived from day to day, and the other providing a long-range overview of these primitive cultures, chapters about remaining artifacts, and listings of locations where these can be viewed by canyon country visitors.

Ms. Michaelene Pendleton, one author, first discovered canyon country in 1954 and has been fascinated by that unique land ever since. Its geology, history and prehistory stimulated a keen interest that drew her back to that wildly eroded, high desert region after sixteen years in Alaska, where in 1972 she acquired a Bachelor of Arts degree in psychology from the University of Alaska. Since then, she has supplemented her degree with studies of history and anthropology, in pursuit of her special interest in ancient western civilizations.

Ms. Pendleton began her writing career while in Alaska. There, her articles on a wide range of subjects, from grizzly bears to ice racing, appeared in various Alaskan newspapers and magazines. She is currently employed by the State of Utah as a counsellor, while pursuing her alternate career of research and writing about prehistoric American Indian cultures.

In presenting her summary of what is now known about canyon country prehistoric Indians, Ms. Pendleton has reconstructed a vital, living picture of them, using a writing style appropriate to this warmly human approach. Thus, her chapter on these prehistoric cultures actually takes the reader back through the centuries to share in the daily lives of the struggling early Americans who peopled the vast Four Corners region from ancient times until about 1300 A.D.

The other author is Mr. F. A. (Fran) Barnes, well known canyon country enthusiast, writer and photographer who has generated eight other books, hundreds of magazine articles and three special maps, all about various aspects of the Four Corners region.

In preparing his introductory overview of the prehistoric canyon country Indian cultures, Mr. Barnes has drawn upon a broad educational background in the physical and human sciences, plus decades of experience at translating complex technical knowledge into written material that can be understood by the average reader.

To prepare his chapters on the various prehistoric cultural remnants that can still be viewed within canyon country, Mr. Barnes has utilized experience gained from more than a decade of continuous exploration of this unique region, and has selected representative pictures of these remnants from his extensive photographic files.

In presenting his material, Mr. Barnes has used the impersonal writing style that he thought appropriate to his subjects: the broad flow of prehistoric American cultures, their surviving remnants, and the destructive clash between the prehistoric, historic and present American cultures.

The book resulting from this collaboration of authors should be of interest to almost anyone with any curiosity about our prehistoric American heritage. It gives a broad view and an intimate view — a look at the unrecorded past, recent history and the present. It examines without qualms the impact between a prehistoric culture and its pitiful remains, and our historic and modern cultures.

In sum, we feel that this book provides a good look at still another aspect of canyon country — its prehistoric Indians — and makes a useful addition to the Canyon Country series of guide books.

The Publisher

ACKNOWLEDGMENTS

I wish gratefully to acknowledge the help I received in illustrating the ARTIFACTS chapter of this book. When I first started organizing the book's contents, I was startled to discover that I had on hand not one single photograph of a prehistoric Indian artifact. For my voluminous photo files to be so completely lacking was most unusual, and my first thought was that I had somehow really been remiss on a very important aspect of canyon country, a land whose every facet I have tried to photograph over the past twelve years.

On second thought, however, I realized that my total lack of prehistoric artifact photos was a direct result of my being one of the few southeastern Utah residents who have never, ever gone out "point and pot hunting." I didn't have any artifact photos because I had never, in all of my many years and thousands of miles in the Four Corners backcountry, collected a prehistoric artifact of any sort. I had violated neither the federal, state nor moral laws that forbid amateur artifact hunting.

With that realization, my dismay changed into a glow of self-congratulation—but that glow did little to illustrate the needed chapter on prehistoric Indian artifacts. My thoughts then turned to consideration of legitimate sources of such photographs.

I am happy to report that two southeastern Utah public agencies have been most cooperative by providing me legally acquired artifacts to photograph for this book. The Moab Museum in Moab, Utah, graciously allowed me to take pictures of items from its displays, and the National Park Service permitted me to photograph representative items from its Canyonlands collection, items that are intended for display at a museum that is now in the early stages of planning. In addition, the University of Utah Archaeological Center provided a number of prints from its files of typical artifacts in its Anasazi and Fremont collections.

I thus extend my sincere thanks to the kind people in these three organizations—city, academic and federal—who contributed to making this book complete. What better reward could I ask for my years of restraint in this land so rich in archaeological treasure?

Fran Barnes

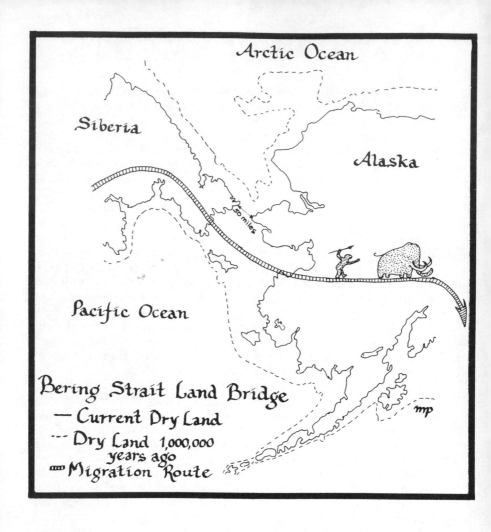

Arctic Ocean

Siberia

Alaska

50 miles

Pacific Ocean

Bering Strait Land Bridge
— Current Dry Land
--- Dry Land 1,000,000
      years ago
▦▦ Migration Route

mp

AN OVERVIEW
by
F. A. Barnes

Cave-wall pictographs above Defiance House ruins, Forgotten Canyon, Glen Canyon National Recreation Area.

9

"All American Man" pictograph, Salt Creek Canyon, Canyonlands National Park, Utah. This large figure is located in a cave and painted with red, white and blue pigments, hence its name.

10

AN OVERVIEW

CANYON COUNTRY

Each book in the "Canyon Country" series defines this term on the basis of the subject matter and scope of the book, using appropriate combinations of natural and man-made geographic features and arbitrary lines.

Defining "canyon country" from the viewpoint of the prehistoric Indians who once occupied vast areas of the Four Corners states of Arizona, Colorado, New Mexico and Utah, was not easy, because archaeologists have yet to establish precise boundaries for these unique early American cultures.

According to local usage of the term, "canyon country," or "canyonlands," is that part of southeastern Utah that the Colorado and Green rivers and their various tributaries have eroded into a vast, complex canyon system over the last ten million years. Geologically, however, this canyon system does not recognize state boundaries. Its heartland lies within southeastern Utah, but it also intrudes into western Colorado, northern Arizona and northwestern New Mexico. Geologists call this region the Colorado Plateau Province.

The prehistoric Indian cultures that occupied the heartland "canyon country" also occupied most of the Colorado Plateau Province, as well as some adjoining areas. See the regional map on the inside front cover for an approximation of how various natural, man-made, geologic and cultural boundaries relate to each other within the general Four Corners region.

For the purposes of this book, then, "canyon country" is defined very broadly, encompassing roughly the entire Colorado Plateau Province, or approximately the entire region occupied by the prehistoric Anasazi and Fremont Indian cultures. For detailed descriptions of this wild, rugged and sparsely occupied region as it is today, refer to other books in the "Canyon Country" series.

FIRST AMERICANS

Anthropologists are widely agreed that the human race originated in the eastern hemisphere, in Africa and Asia, but they do not agree on when and how humanity came to occupy the two major continents of the western hemisphere, North and South America, and their connecting link, Central America.

Archaeologists, those anthropologists who specialize in humanity's long and mysterious pre-history, have found plentiful evidence that the first humans reached the western continents by way of a broad land bridge between Alaska and Siberia that has intermittently linked Asia and North America during the last several million years as the world's sea level has fluctuated.

Indisputable evidence gathered to date indicates that the first major human migration into the Americas took place sometime between 12,000 and 15,000 years ago, although there are some indications of very limited migrations as early as 25,000 to 35,000 years ago.

The migration of some 12,000 to 15,000 years ago is well established, and there is incontestable evidence that beginning about then, humanity spread steadily across most of North and South America. Some scientists point out that this flow of humanity onto two continents previously empty of its species was coincidental with the retreat of a glacial age. This retreat first opened a feasible land route for the migration of certain larger land animals, and for the human hunters who followed these animals. The retreating, melting glaciers then closed the land route by simply raising the world's sea level.

It is well established that the early humans who entered the western hemisphere about 12,000 to 15,000 years ago were subsequently isolated for thousands of years from any contact with humanity in the eastern hemisphere. This isolation imposed genetic limitations upon western hemisphere humanity, but also allowed environmental influences to mold these early Asiatic migrants into the distinct ethnic group known today as American Indians, or "Amerinds," as distinct from the East Indians who occupy the Indian subcontinent of Asia.

Physical anthropologists have found that all Amerinds share certain body characteristics, such as sharply limited blood types, unique skin pigmentation, stocky build, dark eyes, coarse and straight head hair, sparse body hair, rare baldness and graying, and certain anomalies in their fingerprints and teeth. These shared characteristics, and others less obvious, appear to indicate that relatively few people crossed that land bridge some 12,000 to 15,000 years ago, and that these predecessors of the American Indian were isolated for millennia from the main gene pool of humanity in the eastern hemisphere.

Small arrowheads, Canyonlands National Park collection.

There is some evidence that developing Amerind humanity received a minor infusion of Asian traits about 5000 or 6000 years ago, probably via a briefly reopened Siberian-Alaskan land route. There is also some evidence that a primitive seagoing Asiatic culture may have made contact with early Amerinds along the west coast of South America some 2000 or 3000 years ago, but to date this evidence is not conclusive.

Regardless of all the incomplete aspects of humanity's story in the western hemisphere, it is well established that the Asiatic migrants who reached America about 12,000 to 15,000 years ago spread fairly rapidly, although sparsely, across most of North, Central and South America. There, these primitive, Stone Age humans set about adapting to whatever lands they chose to occupy.

The lifestyle these earliest Americans used was the only one they knew, that of hunting and gathering, moving constantly with the wild game and as the seasons affected the plant products they ate. While such a hunting-gathering culture is primitive, hazardous, difficult and virtually unchanging, it has one enormous advantage in a natural environment. No matter how rugged that environment may be, hunting-gathering is a flexible, high survival style of living. It does not encourage the development of "higher" cultural traits or an explosive growth of population, but it does permit survival of the species over a long period of time and through all kinds of natural adversity and change.

The first Americans arrived from Asia as very primitive Stone Age, or "Lithic," savages. As they spread south and east across North America from what is now Alaska, they slowly adapted to the rich, new lands they were occupying, gradually phasing into what archaeologists call the "Archaic" stage of cultural development. The transformation from Lithic to Archaic cultural stage was essentially one of changing from a relatively narrow, limited subsistence base to one that utilized more of the available natural resources.

During the earliest or Lithic stage, these first Americans had few and very primitive tools, and they concentrated more on the larger game animals, possibly because this was the tradition they brought with them from Asia. As they adapted to the new land, however, with its different and perhaps more diverse resources, these early Amerinds developed a much broader subsistence base, using smaller game as well as larger animals, learning to use America's many edible fruits, seeds and other plant products, and developing more complex tools to aid in this diversification.

The first or Lithic stage lasted until about 9000 years ago, although this varied in different parts of the North American continent. Those who occupied the more rugged western region of the continent adapted to the Archaic level first, followed by those in the eastern forestlands. The last to adapt were the occupants of the central plains, perhaps because the big game animals so vital to Lithic tradition were the most abundant there.

CHANGE

The Archaic cultural stage persisted virtually unchanged for thousands of years over the entire North American continent, then something triggered a major cultural phase change in the region that is now Central America, transforming the Amerinds who occupied this tropical region from peripatetic hunter-gatherers into relatively stationary agriculturists. Archaeologists call this next cultural phase the "Formative."

As noted earlier, there is some evidence that the Amerinds in Central America may have been jolted out of their static Archaic stage by infusions of more advanced cultures from across the Pacific Ocean, brought to the western hemisphere by hardy Asiatic seafarers thousands of years before Europeans began sailing westward across the Atlantic Ocean.

Whatever the cause, be it cultural transfusion or spontaneous development, beginning several thousand years ago, the Amerinds of Central America and vicinity moved rapidly from the primitive Archaic culture into the far more sophisticated Formative stage.

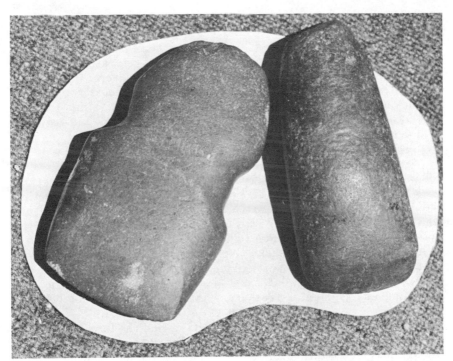

Stone ax heads, Moab Museum collection.

Agriculture, basic to the Formative stage, encouraged innovation in other cultural aspects, including weaponry, clothing, ceramics, religion, handcrafts, architecture and social structure.

Slowly but inevitably, these major new cultural attributes moved northward and eastward from their base in Central America and Mexico, spreading among the sparse inhabitants of North America like slow motion ripples from a stone dropped into water.

Strangely, these slow motion cultural ripples completely by-passed the Archaic stage Indians who occupied what are now northern Mexico, most of Nevada and the Pacific coast states. The Amerinds in this vast far-west region were still in the Archaic stage of development when historic European and Asian explorers first contacted them.

The Formative cultural innovations from Mexico did, however, affect the Archaic stage inhabitants in the general region of the present Four Corners states. There, the introduction of agriculture marked the transition of these ancestors of the "Anasazi" Indians from the nomadic Basketmaker I or "Desert Archaic," cultural level, into the semi-agrarian Basketmaker II phase at about A.D. 1, give or take a century. These and other cultural classifications are discussed in further detail in the last section of the chapter on PREHISTORIC CULTURES, and are illustrated graphically on the inside back cover.

The Archaic predecessors of the Anasazis were a hardy and rugged people, well adapted to survival in a vast region that had been slowly but steadily becoming warmer and more arid over the ten millennia since the last continental glaciers had retreated from what is now the United States. As they accepted the cultural innovations from the south, such as agriculture, ceramics and, later, stonemasonry, textiles and social systems, they adapted these new things to their own local conditions, retaining such regional traditions and traits as food preparation techniques, unique adaptations to the local environment, a classless society and a non-aggressive nature.

Beginning with the Basketmaker II phase, the distinctive Anasazi culture developed steadily for about 1200 years, reaching during its peak at about 1200 A.D. the highest level of cultural attainment that the American Indian was to reach before the native Amerind culture was shattered forever by the influx of European cultures beginning in the 16th century. In contrast to the relatively sophisticated cultural achievements of the Anasazis, the Indian tribes in the eastern and southeastern regions of North America were fairly primitive. The slow-motion cultural ripples from Mexico had not reached them as soon, and environmental pressures for innovation had not been so severe.

Modern Americans, who live at a time when the flow of technical and cultural innovation seems to be southward, from America into Mexico, may find it difficult to believe that not too long ago the flow of innovation was northward, from Mexico to the rest of North America.

And while the great Amerind cultures of South and Central America and Mexico were the highest attained within the western hemisphere, the highest level ever reached by native North Americans was the Anasazi culture of canyon country.

RETREAT

The burgeoning Anasazi culture was not to continue its growth, however. Beginning some time around 1200 A.D., something, or several things, happened that drastically affected the Anasazis and other neighboring cultures in the Four Corners states. At its peak, the Anasazi culture loosely occupied an immense area in the general Four Corners region. To the north of Anasazi territory, the Fremont culture occupied almost all of the rest of what is now Utah, plus a small segment of northwestern Colorado. South of the Anasazis, the Mogollon, Hohokam and other cultures sprawled across most of what are now the states of Arizona and New Mexico. See the regional map on the inside front cover.

By 1250 A.D., these tribal territories had begun to shrink, with the Fremonts and Anasazis losing ground the most rapidly. By 1300 A.D., the Fremonts were essentially gone as a distinctive Formative-

Anasazi cliff-dwelling, San Juan River gorge, Utah.

stage culture, and the Anasazis had completely withdrawn from all their previously thriving settlements and larger communities in Utah and Colorado. They continued to occupy only greatly shrunken regions in northeastern Arizona and central New Mexico.

This massive cultural retreat continued, with significant developmental progress at a virtual standstill, until Spanish explorers first entered the region in 1540 A.D. Although the forceful impact of the Spanish culture on the region's Amerind cultures somewhat muddied the anthropological waters, archaeologists are pretty well agreed that two of the modern Pueblo tribes, the Hopis and Taos, are the direct descendants of the Anasazis, while the neighboring Mogollons and Hohokams became the modern Zuni and Pima-Papago, respectively.

The full story of what happened to the thriving Anasazi, Fremont and adjacent cultures may never be known. There is at present no consensus among archaeologists, although several have suggested possible causes based upon their field research findings.

One archaeologist, who has spent years excavating Anasazi sites in southeastern Utah, proposes that some of the larger Anasazi communities may have committed "ecological suicide," with a little help from changing or varying climate and other factors. By this concept, as the larger, more sophisticated pueblos grew, they used more and more trees for structural purposes, fuel and other uses, slowly denuding nearby forests and thus destroying them as watersheds and sources of game and forage foods. This in turn placed more of a burden on agriculture, which itself suffered from failed springs and streams, plus flash flooding from the destroyed watershed. There is considerable evidence to show that this complex ecological disaster actually happened at some of the larger Anasazi communities.

An anthropologist who is quite familiar with the prehistoric and historic Amerind cultures of the Four Corners region, has proposed that communicable diseases played an important, if not vital, part in the region's drastic cultural retreat during the latter part of the 1200s A.D. He theorizes that once the pueblo culture reached a certain critical stage of development, with the attendant large centers of occupation and fairly regular travel between them, a virulent disease, perhaps inadvertently "imported" from the tropical cultures in southern Mexico, could spread rapidly and disastrously. Certainly, modern medical research has shown that such a cause-and-effect relationship can exist between population density and the rapid spread of contagious diseases.

Other archaeologists have other ideas. One is that prolonged drought over the entire region caused widespread starvation and withdrawal to a few areas that had reliable water sources. Another is that the peaceful, agrarian pueblo tribes were beset by nomadic, warlike raiders from neighboring regions, perhaps as a secondary effect of the drought that is known to have occurred. Or perhaps the pressures from the nomadic tribes, which are known to have invaded from farther west about this time, were in the form of the persistent theft of crops and stored food. Either type of cultural pressure, if prolonged, would have been devastating to the indigenous canyon country cultures.

There is also evidence that in some areas of the region, there was an apparent change from the normal winter rains to destructive summer flash flooding. There is geologic evidence to indicate that there was, indeed, a short range climatic change about that time, with attendant glaciation at elevations above 10,000 feet.

No one of these hypotheses, however, seems to be sufficient explanation for the drastic cultural retreat forced onto the Anasazis, the Fremonts and other nearby Formative-stage cultures. It would be difficult to stretch the ecological suicide concept to fit the hundreds of very small Anasazi settlements, or the less advanced Fremont villages, even though this process probably did affect some of the larger Anasazi communities.

The communicable disease proposal does not explain why the Anasazis abandoned some large pueblos, but not others, nor why the Fremonts seemed to backslide almost completely into the Archaic stage. Tree ring studies have shown that the big drought that did occur in the mid-1200s A.D. was not that much worse than others had been, casting doubt upon the drought hypothesis, at least as the sole cause. And while a climatic shift that brought a change in rainfall pattern would doubtless have caused trouble for a farming culture, generally such climatic shifts occur slowly, over centuries, and farmers over the ages simply grin-and-bear-it with short-range weather vagaries.

The idea of severe pressures of one sort or another from more primitive tribes from farther west has considerable merit, since it has been well demonstrated throughout all of human history that mankind is usually its own worst enemy. Even so, there is little evidence to support the idea of numerous armed attacks and mass slaughter. Many Anasazi settlements were simply abandoned, without any signs of violence. Nor does the concept of food and crop raids seem to be enough to explain the complete destruction of the Fremont culture, and the enormous loss of population and mass exodus to a few small areas that mark the Anasazi territorial retreat.

Time and further research may reveal a clear-cut cause for this strange cultural phenomenon, but in all probability this cause will prove to be multi-faceted, a complex, interrelated blend of several different effects, some now known, others yet to be discovered.

Hungo Pavie ruins, Chaco Canyon National Monument, New Mexico.

HIATUS

Following the abrupt withdrawal of the Anasazi culture in the southern part of canyon country, and the dissolution of the less advanced Fremont culture in the northern part of the region, there was a cultural hiatus of several hundred years in most of canyon country. The remnants of the Anasazis occupied the Rio Grande Valley in north-central New Mexico and three smaller areas farther west, while the surviving Fremonts integrated into other surrounding Archaic-stage cultures.

This exodus left most of the extensive Anasazi-Fremont region empty of permanent inhabitants. Bordering tribes entered the region solely for hunting and foraging. In the northern part of the region, in most of what is now Utah and southwestern Colorado, this cultural hiatus persisted into the late 1800s A.D., when white explorers and settlers first entered the area.

In the southern part of canyon country, however, the vast expanses of land the Anasazis had abandoned soon attracted another more primitive people, the predecessors of the Navajo and Apache tribes. Anthropologists who specialize in languages believe that these southward-drifting nomads were of Athabascan stock, from northwestern Canada and the Alaska interior. The route these invaders of canyon country took has not been fully determined, but some archaeologists believe they traveled southward through the game-rich Rocky Mountain range, to disperse into the Four Corners region and on south.

This new cultural wave entering the southern part of canyon country was still essentially in the Archaic, or non-agricultural, phase. Even so, the tough tribesmen who moved into the territory vacated by the Anasazis were better armed than the peaceful, agrarian Anasazis. Further, the invaders were quite aggressive and warlike, with a curious cultural propensity for "borrowing" from other tribes. Their borrowing included food, women and any cultural traits that seemed useful.

This, in turn, put further pressures upon the remaining Anasazi enclaves. As a result, Anasazi territory shrank still more. By 1700 A.D., despite still further pressures from Spanish explorers and colonists, the descendants of the Anasazis still occupied their Rio Grande Valley pueblos and several other areas to the west, while the Navajo Indians, as the cultural invaders who remained in canyon country came to be called, claimed most of the rest of the region. Despite a series of treaties imposed upon these two disparate cultures by white men, the territorial dispute between them continues even today, a dispute that is rooted in more than 500 years of cultural antipathy.

REMNANTS

The retreat of the Anasazi culture from the immense region occupied during its heyday, and the dispersal of the Fremonts from their almost equally large territory, left behind a whole spectrum of cultural remnants, from great cliff dwellings to remote, seasonal hunting camps; from heaps of broken pottery to thousands of panels of rock art; from graves filled with human bones and artifacts to isolated sites where religious ceremonies took place.

As time passed, these cultural remnants slowly yielded to the elements, although the semi-arid climate that dominates the general Four Corners region is far less destructive to archaeological sites than the wetter climate in other parts of the country. On the whole, the region's drier, desert climate, together with the resulting sparse vegetation, rugged terrain and late development by our current culture, tended to preserve the Anasazi and Fremont remnants quite well. The remains of early Amerind cultures in the richer, more quickly developed parts of America have not fared very well at all.

Strangely, the Archaic culture that invaded the land deserted by the Anasazis did little or nothing to destroy the Anasazi remnants left behind. The ancestral Navajos used the land as hunters, foragers and herdsmen. They tended to avoid the visible remnants of those who had occupied the land before them, perhaps out of superstition, or perhaps because they had no desire to occupy the ecologic niche favored by the Anasazis.

Whatever the reason, the Navajos did very little to hasten the slow, natural disintegration of the cultural remnants of the Anasazis, and the Fremonts left so little tangible when they dispersed that the few hunters who subsequently entered their region probably saw little trace of earlier human occupancy.

Early Spanish explorers who encountered the descendants of the Anasazi culture in Arizona and New Mexico in the mid-1500s A.D. had a devastating impact upon that relatively static Formative-stage enclave of American Indians. Later Spanish exploration parties that entered what are now Colorado and Utah, such as the famed Dominguez-Escalante expedition of 1776, saw little of the prehistoric remnants of the Anasazis and Fremonts, even though their exploring routes did penetrate the very heart of the regions these cultures had formerly occupied. This is not surprising, of course. The Spanish were looking for feasible routes through that rugged, canyon-slashed region, and living natives they could convert to Christianity, not long-abandoned prehistoric settlements located in remote cliffs and canyons.

Thus, although two major cultures, ancestral-Navajo and Spanish, invaded and to some extent occupied the abandoned territories of the Anasazis and Fremonts for hundreds of years, the remnants of these cultures that had been left behind remained largely intact, undamaged by mankind and only lightly affected by the arid desert climate. Then white men, modern Americans, entered the scene.

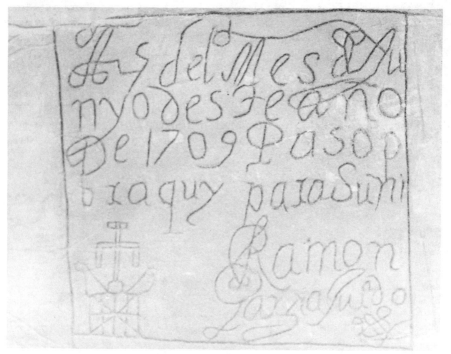

Inscription left by an early Spanish explorer, El Morro National Monument, New Mexico. Note the 1709 date.

DISCOVERY

The first impact of our modern American culture upon the remnants of the Anasazi and Fremont cultures was gentle, and barely noticeable outside of a few scholarly circles. Early exploring parties into the unmapped Four Corners region, such as the Macomb Expedition of 1859 and the Powell Expeditions of 1869 and 1871, reported finding strange rock constructions in unlikely places, but these reports went largely unheeded by archaeologists.

The Hayden-Jackson geologic survey of the mid-1870s also reported prehistoric ruins in the Four Corners region of Utah, as did early Mormon scouts and settlers who pioneered southeastern Utah about the same time. But again, these little-publicized findings escaped general notice, and the ancient Anasazi-Fremont domain continued to be terra incognita to contemporary America. The newly burgeoning Euro-American culture had yet to find and recognize the remnants of what had been the highest native American culture.

Then, in 1889, the Wetherills, a family of ranchers in the Four Corners area, brought this archaeological treasury to the attention of the outside world by publicizing a series of discoveries, among them the spectacular cliff dwellings of Mesa Verde in Colorado, and by collecting and selling quantities of prehistoric artifacts from the sites they found. While such flagrant sales of antiquities now would quickly earn the culprits a stiff fine, and perhaps a prison term as well, in the unenlightened days of the late 1800s there simply were no laws protecting America's precious prehistoric heritage.

It might be said, then, that for better or worse, the Wetherills initiated modern America's impact upon the remnants of the prehistoric Anasazi and Fremont cultures. This impact, more destructive than instructive, grew steadily from the dawn of the 20th century until the 1940s. Then it accelerated still further, until it has now reached an appalling level of devastation. Unless this devastation is soon slowed or halted, by the turn of the next century pitifully little will remain of the highest native-American culture that will ever exist.

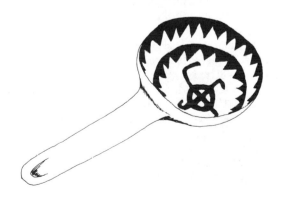

Anasazi cliff-dwelling, Mesa Verde National Park, Colorado.

EARLY IMPACT

The blatant commercial exploitation of the newly discovered Anasazi cliff dwellings and other sites, by the Wetherills and others, continued for more than a decade. During this tragic interval, enormous quantities of invaluable artifacts were stripped from the ruins of what remained of the highest cultural attainment of native Americans. Terrible damage was done to the structures that still survived, as the commercial collectors excavated site after site, heedless of anything but the saleable loot they could carry away.

This incredible period of theft and destruction irreversibly blurred the cultural picture left for archaeologists to study when a hardy few eventually did manage to reach some of the major ruins of the general Four Corners region.

Shortly after the turn of the century, public and scientific outrage over the systematic commercial looting of the Anasazi ruins finally reached Congress. Thus, a federal antiquities law was enacted that at least provided theoretical legal protection to archaeological sites and other antiquities on federal land. Dated June 8, 1906, it was titled "An Act for the Preservation of American Antiquities."

This overdue law was brief, and quite ambiguous concerning "antiquities" other than archaeological. Although covered by the 1906 law in principle, such valuable antiquities as paleontological and paleobotanical specimens — fossilized animal and plant remains — have received virtually no protection. The brief act did restrict the "examination of ruins, the excavation of archaeological sites and the gathering of objects of antiquity" upon federal land to "reputable museums, universities, colleges, or other recognized scientific or educational institutions," and the original enforcing regulations issued by the Secretaries of Agriculture, Interior and War echoed this mandate.

At the enforcement level, however, this clear mandate to protect America's priceless heritage of antiquities had two major flaws that virtually negated any value the Antiquities Act might have had. The Act applied only to federally owned or controlled land, leaving antiquities located on vast expanses of private and state lands still open to exploitation and destruction. Eventually, most states enacted similar laws, but some delayed this vital step for decades. Utah, for example, failed to enact an effective law until 1973, a classic case of locking the barn door long after most of the horses have been stolen.

The second major flaw in the practical enforcement of the 1906 Antiquities Act was the fact that few within the federal government really wanted to enforce it. While the Act did contain a broad mandate for federal land administration agencies to protect all antiquities, it had really been aimed at the commercial looters whose behavior had so enraged a large number of voters. The Act did put a stop to the more flagrant looting and destruction of this sort, but in practice afforded little if any protection to archaeological and other antiquities sites from the more surreptitious commercial and hobby collectors, or from the massive destruction from industrial development that came later. Congress underscored its casual interest in the matter by simply not funding any practical protection efforts in the field, and this attitude was inevitably reflected within all levels of the three major federal land administration agencies.

Thus, for the more than three-quarters of a century that the 1906 Antiquities Act has theoretically been in force, the practical effect this law has had on the protection of antiquities of all sorts in the Four Corners region has been minimal. The various archaeological teams that have done research in the region have observed its provisions, but few others have. Until very recently, even the federal land administration agencies, with a few exceptions such as the National Park Service, have virtually ignored the law, and their current regulations implementing the 1906 Antiquities Act contain highly questionable interpretations of such critical terms in the original Act as "objects of antiquity."

25

RECENT IMPACT

After the Antiquities Act of 1906 put an abrupt halt to the more flagrant commercial collection and destruction of Anasazi cultural remnants, this practice continued at a less obvious level. Private and commercial collectors still hunted "pots" and "points" and dug in ruins, encouraged by the obvious fact that Congress had not really meant the Act to be fully enforced, and that this indifferent attitude also prevailed at all levels within federal land administration agencies.

Many archaeological sites on private land were stripped of all scientific value during the succeeding decades, and a few were even developed into commercial "tourist traps." Vast commercial agricultural developments in the Four Corners region destroyed innumerable archaeological sites, while the value of countless other sites was severely diminished by local animal husbandry practices.

Antiquities on the huge blocks of state land that checkerboard federal land in the Four Corners states received little more practical protection from exploitation and damage than those on private land. While some states paid lip service to the concept of protecting archaeological sites, enforcement was nullified by low or non-existent budgets for that purpose, and by the simple fact that most archaeological sites were in remote locations within wild and terribly broken terrain, and thus difficult to protect.

Enforcement of antiquities laws was also hampered by the curious fact that thousands of archaeological sites were located within the several huge Indian reservations that sprawl across the general Four Corners region, creating an enforcement "gray area." Technically, Indian reservations are under the jurisdiction of the federal Bureau of Indian Affairs, and hence are "owned or controlled by" the federal government. Thus, they fall under the 1906 Antiquities Act. But for practical purposes, the Act was not enforced on reservations. While the Indians, themselves, largely ignored or avoided the countless archaeological sites on their lands, just as they had for hundreds of years, the mining and energy industries that were licensed to operate on their reservations were highly destructive.

As the destruction and exploitation of prehistoric Anasazi and Fremont sites continued on private and reservation lands, the states also cooperated in similar destruction of archaeological values on state lands by the outright sale of land into private ownership, by land exchanges with industrial and other land developers, and by the granting of land leases for agricultural and other uses that jeopardize or destroy archaeological sites.

Further, the states promoted the wholesale destruction of archaeological sites on land still under state jurisdiction by pursuing such questionable "range management" practices as "chaining." This is a process in which huge tracts of wooded land are cleared of forestation by dragging heavy steel anchor chain between large bulldozers.

Anasazi cliff-dwelling ruin, Lavender Canyon, Canyonlands National Park, Utah. Illegal digging has severely damaged this ruin.

This uproots and kills all the trees and larger shrubs, theoretically improving grazing for domestic livestock. It also destroys any archaeological sites that are hidden within the chained area. Within the last several decades Utah, for example, has chained many thousands of acres of pinion-juniper forestland within the region formerly occupied by the Anasazi-Fremont cultures. Few, if any, efforts were made to survey such areas for archaeological value before chaining, or to salvage anything of this nature found during the chaining.

Federal land administration agencies, with the exception of the National Park Service, also tacitly or actively cooperated in the continuing devastation of prehistoric remnants within the Four Corners region. They bowed to political pressures from the states by granting land exchanges that involved numerous archaeological sites. One such exchange on record justified the exchange on the basis that there were no sites found on a 7000 acre tract, even though such sites had been found in many places nearby. The "environmental analysis" released before the exchange noted that the archaeological survey had been performed during a certain month, a month in which only local residents knew that the area "surveyed" had been under several feet of snow, making a field survey impossible.

The two federal agencies that administer more than half of the land in the Four Corners region, the U.S. Forest Service and the Bureau of Land Management, also chained vast areas of land known to be high in archaeological potential. Typically, if surveys for these values were made at all in advance of the chaining, they were done hastily and by completely unqualified individuals, such as a local cowboy on horseback. And if even these cursory surveys found a few obvious sites, these were shrugged off as "unimportant." Since the dubious range management practice of chaining first came into use within the Four Corners states, federal land administration agencies have chained tens of thousands of acres of forestland, forever obliterating all surface traces of any archaeological sites these areas may have held. Many of those chained areas were within regions known to be rich in archaeological value.

Federal land administration agencies also cooperated in archaeological destruction by establishing thousands of miles of "utility corridors" across federal land, without adequate prior surveys for archaeological sites.

Such cynical flouting of the 1906 Antiquities Act by the federal agencies charged with its enforcement, and by state land administration agencies, has resulted in incalculable losses to the limited and irreplaceable remnants of the prehistoric Anasazi and Fremont cultures. Such losses, together with other huge losses from early looting, plus the continuing losses on private lands, have severely hampered the efforts of modern archaeologists to piece together meaningful pictures of these cultures.

It is a sad commentary on America's level of cultural sophistication that the government agencies who are charged by law with protecting and preserving American antiquities are, instead, by their actions and inactions, the greatest destroyers of these antiquities.

A "chained" pinyon-juniper forest in the foothills of the Abajo Mountains, Utah, an area that is rich in archaeological sites.

ARCHAEOLOGICAL RESEARCH

The first serious attempts at archaeological research in the Four Corners region began early in the 1900s, but were largely directed toward a general inventory of the better known sites. The succeeding decades were marked more by scientific neglect and indifference than by any concerted effort to accept the challenge of studying the prehistoric cultures of canyon country. A few competent but quite limited studies were made, and many individual sites were excavated, but there were no overall, regional surveys of the Anasazi and Fremont cultural remnants. While a few American archaeologists became interested in the region's human prehistory, most were concerned with other areas of study.

Funds for field research in canyon country were rare, whether from universities, foundations, the government, or private sources. Strangely, the most fascinating, highly developed prehistoric native-American culture was being devastated by impact with our modern American culture, with barely a whimper of protest or a surge of activity from the academic world.

Although a few dedicated researchers have taken a keen, lifelong interest in the Anasazi-Fremont cultures, and have contributed greatly toward the slowly growing body of knowledge about these unique early Americans, field research on this subject continues to be sporadic at best, and only fitfully financed by the government agencies and state universities that by law have cognizance over such research.

Most of the field research that is performed is in the form of crash program "salvage" operations that are belatedly set up to save whatever can be found quickly, before some immense industrial project destroys all archaeological values in an area, or along a route. The construction of Glen Canyon Dam and the creation of Lake Powell initiated one such salvage project. The construction of Flaming Gorge Reservoir was another. Although these efforts did save a considerable amount of artifacts and knowledge from total loss, there is little doubt that far more was lost, irretrievably, than was salvaged. The reservoir waters simply inundated too many hundreds of miles of deep and rugged canyons for a short-range survey or salvage operation to handle in any but the most superficial manner. Thus, while the glistening, blue waters of Flaming Gorge Reservoir and Lake Powell are beautiful to behold, they are also the dark graveyards for vast archaeological treasures that are now lost to humanity forever.

Other archaeological salvage operations, such as for highways and other construction projects, have sometimes fared better, but there is little doubt that for each site salvaged, many others are lost. One thing learned from actual field research projects is that in almost every case, more sites are found than were suspected. From this it is easy to conclude that losses due to modern "progress" are always far greater than claimed by the developers.

Small Anasazi cliff-dwelling, Lake Canyon, Glen Canyon National Recreation Area, before the reservoir filled.

The same ruin as the reservoir waters intruded into the canyon. The ruin is now under water.

In sum, it could be said that the history of the impact of our modern American culture upon the prehistoric Amerind cultures of canyon country is a strange mixture of fascinating discovery, raw greed, mystifying neglect, tragic loss, cursory surveys, unique findings, scientific preoccupation, personal dedication, inexplicable mysteries, public apathy, intensive research, unenforced laws, scholastic disinterest, political cynicism, administrative inertia, industrial indifference, exotic hypotheses, and appalling destruction. This baffling exhibition of cultural ambiguity continues even now.

PRESENT SITUATION

Within the second half of the 1970s decade, there has been a significant increase in public interest in America's prehistory. This interest has, in turn, sparked belated government efforts to identify, record and protect the rapidly dwindling remnants of this prehistory.

At the same time, however, in canyon country at least, any gains made by such protective efforts have been more than offset by explosive growth among the destructive forces that jeopardize what remains of the prehistoric Anasazi and Fremont cultures. Thus, the future looks even grimmer than the past with respect to saving these remnants.

Thoroughgoing, scientific archaeological field research projects within canyon country continue to be infrequent, sporadic and not a part of any integrated, overall survey. Some very productive, long range university field projects have been discontinued for lack of funding. Most ongoing academic research is concerned with a few major sites, most of them already well protected within federal park areas, and is generally confined to literary and laboratory work, with minimal new field effort.

Past academic efforts have at least recorded and partially studied all the known major sites, but literally hundreds of lesser sites known to exist have never been studied at all, and no overall, comprehensive archaeological survey of the entire canyon country region is in sight. In 1971, federal land administration agencies were ordered to inventory all federal lands for archaeological and other sites that might qualify for listing as National Historic Places. More recent orders for wilderness surveys have further emphasized the need for surveying federal lands for antiquities. Unfortunately, to date these required surveys have neither been funded nor organized to produce more than superficial results. In some cases, inventories have been made of all previously known and reported sites, but virtually nothing is being done to survey the land itself for the thousands of sites that undoubtedly still remain undiscovered.

Archaeological salvage operations are continuing to gather limited data, but the accelerating need for such operations means still more permanent losses in the salvaged areas. The McPhee reservoir to be built on the Dolores River in southwestern Colorado in the Mesa Verde vicinity, will doubtless mean the permanent loss of still another huge body of knowledge, even though the University of Colorado is attempting to salvage what it can with limited time and funds. Near the site of this dam, a restored and stabilized early pueblo dwelling site will be open to visitor viewing, a public relations gesture that is supposed to compensate the American public for the hundreds of archaeological sites that will be lost forever beneath the reservoir waters.

Despite new state laws, and new federal orders enforcing the federal Antiquities Act of 1906, both federal and state land administration agencies continue to permit the destruction of archaeological sites, and even to perform such destruction themselves. Both federal and state agencies continue to cooperate with industrial, commercial and agricultural developments that destroy archaeological sites wholesale, and both still plan, fund and perform "range improvement" operations such as chaining that forever obliterate any surface signs of prehistoric remnants.

Further, both federal and state land agencies have still failed to issue regulations that impose enough control over mineral search and development operations to protect archaeological values on public land.

Utah's new antiquities law, while excellent in theory, has yet to have much effect in the field. It has encouraged various state agencies, such as the highway department, to consider antiquities during their operations, but has had little effect upon other destructive users of state land.

The illegal collection of prehistoric artifacts in canyon country, for both hobby and commercial purposes, continues virtually unabated. Local residents still pursue their "point and pot" searches, proudly displaying their findings at local hobby shows. Appallingly large private collections of artifacts continue to grow. Commercial collectors continue to buy and sell prehistoric artifacts. Many openly display them, or offer them for sale at local retail outlets, secure in their knowledge that antiquities laws are still not really being enforced.

Three factors encourage and sustain this cynical violation of the law by both hobbyists and commercial collectors. One is the continuing bulldozing of roads and trails into remote, previously roadless regions of canyon country by mineral search activities. Another is the rapidly growing use of off-highway vehicles to travel the many roads and trails built by the mineral industry, and hence reach remote archaeological sites. The third factor is economic. The price that can be obtained for prehistoric artifacts has grown astronomically over the last decade.

In recent years, still another hazard to archaeological sites in canyon country has shifted from minor to major. While past and present collectors have done tremendous damage to canyon country archaeological sites, their motives have generally been personal gain.

Now, however, canyon country archaeological sites are suffering from a different type of damage — vandalism, pure destruction — with no visible motive. Rock walls within ruins that have withstood the ravages of centuries of time are pushed over. Rock art panels are defaced with steel tools or spray paint or bullets.

Land administration agencies have given many known archaeological sites such special designations as "primitive area" or "historical site" in an effort to protect them, but such special designations seemingly serve only to attract vandals, unless the sites are physically guarded by ranger patrols. Even then, some collecting and vandalism continues.

These badly vandalized Fremont pictographs are in Buckhorn Wash within the San Rafael Swell in Utah. Note the numerous bullet holes in and around the larger figure, and the false dates on the spray-painted names.

It has been conjectured that since not even the Archaic-age savages who coexisted for centuries with these cultural remains deliberately destroyed or defaced them, our modern-age vandals must be a strange, new type of genetic throwback to some sub-human level that delights in mindless destruction for its own sake. There would seem to be no other explanation for such irrational behavior.

There is, however, one bright spot in the field of canyon country archaeological research. A few scientists are now attempting to do basic research on the previously neglected field of prehistoric rock art. Such pioneering researchers are aided by the fact that canyon country rock art is notoriously difficult to collect. It generally occurs on huge sandstone boulders or solid cliffs. Vandals can and do deface such primitive graphic efforts, but collectors are baffled. Thus, a high proportion of all the rock art that even existed in canyon country is still there, damaged, perhaps, but still available for study. In contrast, most archaeological sites such as dwellings were stripped bare of artifacts, long before any archaeologist got near them. Rarely have archaeologists been the first to see an above-ground dwelling site just as its prehistoric owner left it.

In sum, the present situation is one of continuing loss of the cultural remnants of prehistoric canyon country Indians. The major destroyers are dams, utility corridors, highways, and residential subdivisions; commercial, industrial and agricultural developments; range improvement projects, logging, mineral exploration and development; and collecting and vandalism.

At present, the archaeological picture of the Anasazi and Fremont cultures is incomplete, and scientists who are concerned with this region fear that their picture will never be completed unless the present destruction of cultural remnants is halted very soon. All this would take is the effective enforcement of present laws, but this is not yet within sight.

AMATEUR EXPLORING

As noted earlier, the roads and trails being built by the mineral industry within canyon country are being used by hobbyists and collectors to reach and strip prehistoric sites. On the positive side, however, these same access routes are also being used by an increasing number of people who recognize and appreciate the value of such sites.

Some of these amateur archaeologists simply study what they find. Others may also attempt to contribute to the known body of knowledge by reporting their findings to the proper authorities. In the past, such public-spirited reporting was largely a waste of time. Even at present, it may not afford the site any protection or stimulate professional scientific study, but at least the conscientious citizen will have done his duty.

At a minimum, new archaeological finds should be reported to the appropriate land administration agency, if the site is on public land. Since any particular spot within canyon country may be on private, state or federal land, and under any of several state or federal agencies, the best place to start such a report is at the nearest office of the federal Bureau of Land Management. There, land ownership maps will help determine who has jurisdiction over the discovery site.

The next step is to report to the indicated federal or state agency or, if the site is on private land, to the owner and the appropriate state historical society. The BLM office can provide the necessary addresses. If an amateur explorer wishes to ensure that a discovery on public land is not lost somewhere in the bureaucratic shuffle, he would be wise to report the finding to three authorities, i.e., the land administration agency, the state historical society, and the state university.

In most of this nation, amateur explorers are not apt to encounter the problem of how to report an archaeological discovery, but canyon country is huge and still largely unexplored by archaeologists for archaeological values. Even the most casual amateur explorer has a fair chance of finding some trace of the region's prehistoric inhabitants that has never before been reported. No doubt, many such sites have been seen by individual cattlemen and prospectors, but such discoveries are valueless unless they are properly reported.

Conscientious amateur explorers have played an important part in the field of canyon country archaeology, and will continue to in the future, so long as they limit themselves to finding, studying, recording and reporting, and do not join the ranks of the collectors and vandals. No responsible American would knowingly take or destroy something that might provide a clue to one of the many cultural mysteries that still remain to be solved in canyon country.

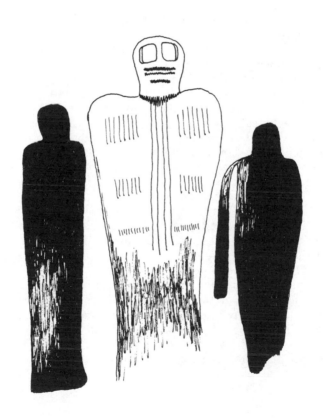

THIS BOOK

This book attempts to provide its readers and canyon country visitors an understanding of the prehistoric Anasazi and Fremont cultures that once occupied this immense and spectacular region, plus a representative look at some of the remnants of these cultures that so far have survived the onslaught of our contemporary culture.

The first chapter presents a look at these cultures themselves, as reconstructed by archaeologists from the research data they have accumulated to date. The chapter's introduction describes some of the problems encountered in presenting this picture.

At the end of the first chapter, one special section describes how archaeologists define some of the sub-groups within the Anasazis and Fremonts, and another describes the cultural calendar shown on the inside back cover of this book.

The next three chapters of the book discuss the three main categories of cultural remnants that archaeologists use in their studies of canyon country prehistoric cultures. These are the Anasazi and Fremont ruins, artifacts and rock art.

The chapter on each of these categories of remnants provides an introduction to the subject, a list of places where canyon country visitors can view representative displays of such remnants, and a number of photographs of typical remnants.

The final chapter notes some of the scientific books and papers used by this book's authors as research sources, and provides a list of books written in a more popular vein that are recommended for further non-technical reading. In addition to the literature sources noted, the authors have drawn upon knowledge and understanding acquired from many hours of personal conversation with anthropologists, archaeologists and other scientists who have specialized in canyon country, and upon many years of experience in the hinterlands of this vast region as amateur archaeologists.

Readers will note that in the chapters on ruins and rock art, the exact locations of specific sites are given only when the sites are well known or in protected locations. The locations of many of the sites shown in the photographs are given only in a general way, because they are still unprotected.

Serious students of such prehistoric cultural remnants are invited to contact the author of the chapters on ruins and rock art for the precise locations of the sites depicted, and many others too, if their studies require a more detailed examination than the photographs provide. This author has on file many hundreds of photographs of ruins and rock art. These are available for scientific use.

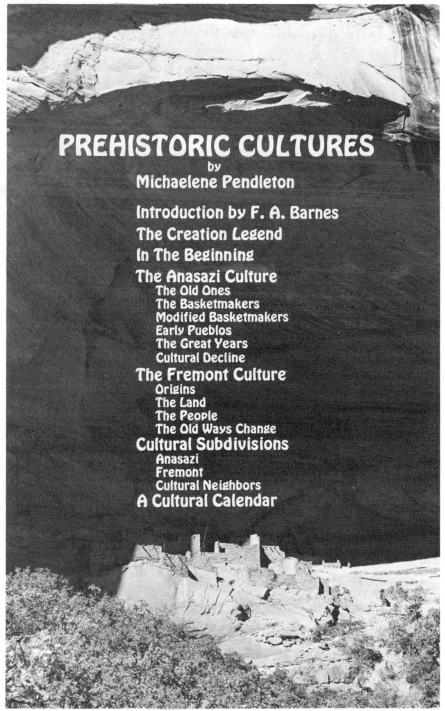

PREHISTORIC CULTURES
by
Michaelene Pendleton

Betatakin Ruin, Navajo National Monument, Arizona.

INTRODUCTION

All branches of science are in a constant state of change, as existing facts are newly analyzed, new facts are revealed by further research, older ideas are revised or discarded, and new ones are devised.

Archaeology, the study of humanity before recorded history, is no exception. In fact, because of the difficulties inherent in archaeological research, and the very limited information with which archaeologists must often work, this branch of the general science of anthropology, or the study of all mankind, may seem to be even more changeable than the branches of science that are more susceptible to careful experimental research.

All too often, archaeologists are faced with the choice of either recording some curious field discovery without comment or evaluation, or of devising an hypothesis, or educated guess, that might possibly explain the finding. They generally make the educated guess.

Thus, at any point in time, archaeological literature is a confusion of differing and even contradictory hypotheses about various subjects. This is especially true of subjects on which relatively limited field research has been done using the latest scientific methodology.

Unfortunately, this situation applies to the special subject of the archaeology of the prehistoric Indian cultures of the general Four Corners region, or "canyon country," a region the size of New Mexico in area, and so wild and rugged and unknown that study of its human prehistory has lagged far behind that in other parts of North America.

Although there are hundreds of research papers on the subject of canyon country prehistoric Indian cultures, most of these are based upon field research done decades ago, when research methods were far less sophisticated. Hypotheses about the Indian cultures drawn from this limited information are often at odds with later findings. There are very few recent scientific papers that attempt to synthesize all existing research data, evaluate it by modern standards and then formulate an overall, integrated picture of the Indian cultures that dominated the vast Four Corners region during the dim prehistory of this unique and least known area in America.

Thus, an author who attempts to perform this task faces a real challenge—to present a picture of these cultures that considers all known facts, and that uses what seem to be the strongest current hypotheses to tie these facts together into an overall pattern.

No matter who performs this difficult task, or what the final picture of the Indian cultures, there will be ample room for disagreement with what the author has produced. Readers of this chapter on the prehistoric Indian cultures of canyon country should understand that at this point in time, all attempts to provide an overview of these cultures are speculative, whether in scientific reports, or in books for popular reading. Actual field research data are still too limited to serve as the basis for any final pronouncements about these ancient cultures.

The images of these cultures presented in this chapter are based upon what is now known about them, and upon current hypotheses — educated guesses — that attempt to weave these facts into a coherent pattern. The author was sometimes forced to choose between conflicting ideas in reports by different archaeologists. Only time and further research will tell which of the differing ideas was correct.

Some of the many reports used in researching this book are listed under "SOURCES" at the end of this book. A few of these reports are quite old, but the actual field data in them are still valid, even though modern field methods might have extracted still more data from the same sites. Although many of the hypotheses in these older reports have been invalidated by later findings, others have been strengthened by further research.

The reader of this chapter on canyon country prehistoric cultures is thus asked to bear in mind that the picture of these cultures presented here merely represents a state-of-the-art image, one that will doubtless change with time. Archaeology is not a static science, and the archaeology of the prehistoric cultures of canyon country is relatively young, with a long, rewarding future ahead as field research continues.

Fran Barnes

Part of the largest pictograph panel in the Horseshoe Canyon Annex of Canyonlands National Park. Note that the painted figures are life-sized or larger.

THE CREATION LEGEND

In the Beginning, there was a great nothingness, a blackness without space or time. And then there was Tawa, the Creator, whose power was the Sun. Out of the blackness, Tawa created all the stars and planets of the Universe, and He created the Earth. And so the Earth would not be alone, Tawa reached deep inside the Earth and planted insect creatures, ants and beetles, and things that crawl.

Mockingbird gave them Tawa's laws and told them of his desires. But the insect creatures didn't understand how Tawa wanted them to live. They fought and quarrelled among themselves. This displeased and sorrowed Tawa so He sent Spider Grandmother to show the insect creatures the way to a better world so that they might live as Tawa wanted.

Spider Grandmother showed the way to a new world Tawa had created closer to the surface of the Earth. As they came into this new world, some of the creatures found that their bodies had changed. Now some of them were wolves, rabbits, coyotes, bear, deer, and all the other animals that live on Earth. But they still didn't understand what Great Tawa wanted, and again they fought and killed each other. Again Tawa sent Spider Grandmother to them.

This time Spider Grandmother led all the animal creatures to a third world that lay just below the surface of the Earth. In this world, some of the animals became men and these Spider Grandmother taught how to live in peace, to plant corn, and to worship Tawa and all the lesser gods.

For a time, all was good and Tawa was pleased. But there were sorcerers among the people, evil men who tempted them away from the life Tawa wanted them to live. The people started to spend their time stealing and gambling, fighting and killing. They neglected their work and they no longer worshipped the gods. But a few of the people did not follow the evil sorcerers. They tended their crops and made their prayer sticks and lived peacefully with each other.

When Tawa saw what was happening, for a third time He sent Spider Grandmother to them. She led the people who had resisted evil up to a small opening in the world. As the people came out of this *sipapu* hole onto the surface of the Earth into the light of Tawa's Sun, Mockingbird changed them into all the different people that now live on Earth. Some were Hopi, some Zuni, some White Men — and they all went their different directions to live as Tawa decreed in the valleys and forests and mountains of the Earth.

So say the Hopi. The legend has lived in the smoke of *kiva* fires since before the memory of the oldest man. It is a tale passed down from the Ancient Ones — the Anasazi.

Sipapu Natural Bridge, in Natural Bridges National Monument, Utah, was named because of its resemblance to the "sipapu" hole in the Hopi legend.

IN THE BEGINNING

Our world was not always as we know it today. More than 25,000 years ago the deserts of the Southwest were cool, rainy places of great forests and rolling plains. It was a larger world, then. No highways or fences bound the land into small parcels, no cities shortened its horizons. But it wasn't an empty place. The mammoth and mastodon shuffled their way across the plains; sabre-toothed cats, cave bears and wolves preyed upon horses the size of dogs; camels and giant bison browsed among the forests. And following these beasts, hunting them and being hunted by them, was man.

As the last great Ice Age was ending, the animals of Asia began to move northward up the coast of what are now China and Siberia, following the cool climate to which they were accustomed. They crossed the land bridge that existed in the Bering Strait between modern-day Russia and Alaska. Over a period of thousands of years the herds, and the predators that followed them, moved south down the western coast of Canada, skirting the small glaciers that still sheeted the interior, until finally they reached the American Southwest.

Prehistoric men were daring hunters. Armed only with flint-tipped spears, they went after the largest land mammal of all time — the mammoth, a huge wooly ancestor of the elephant that sported 10-foot-long tusks. We know they successfully hunted mammoths because mammoth skeletons have been found with spearpoints stuck in their ribs.

Those early hunters were small, nomadic tribesmen who knew nothing of farming or building. They moved with the animal migrations, depending on meat and what berries and roots they could find for their survival. We know very little about them. All they have left behind are a very few skeletons, the bones of the animals they killed, and spearpoints and arrowheads. But from those sparse beginnings arose the civilizations that have bewitched modern man — the Mound Builders, the Aztec and Maya, the Anasazi. By our standards they were savage and uncivilized, but they had adapted to their world.

Then disaster struck. About 8,000 to 10,000 years ago, the giant animals began to die out. Camels and horses which originated on this continent and migrated to Asia, vanished. We can't be sure of the reasons, but the climate, heralding the end of a major glacial epoch, was probably one of the deciding factors. The weather gradually changed from cool and rainy to hot and dry. The Great American desert began to appear. The prehistoric hunters probably helped this extinction. In our own time we have seen the end of the passenger pigeon and most of the buffalo because of our lust to kill. Pleistocene man was no different. Many "mass kill" sites have been found where the ground was littered with the bones of dead animals — many more than could possibly have been eaten by one small tribe. All this was too much for the giant mammals and they disappeared. The smaller mammals which survived moved north and the hunting tribes followed.

But some stayed behind. These were a different kind of people. They had learned to build very crude shelters and they depended on small animals — rabbits and birds — for their food supply. They learned how to forage for berries, seeds, nuts, roots — and most importantly, to store these foods against future need.

The hunters left spearpoints behind them. Now, spearpoints are quite useful, but they aren't far removed from the sharp stick that one chimpanzee will brandish at another. A spearpoint simply evens out the odds when you're hunting something that has teeth and claws. It isn't a foundation of civilization — it isn't a *tool.* The two requirements for building a civilization are tools and a steady food supply. These

42

Visitor center and museum, Edge of the Cedars State Historical Monument, Blanding, Utah.

Small pot, Moab Museum collection.

Anasazi skull with some scalp hair, Moab Museum collection.

43

early people developed both.

The first archaeological evidence of these people was found near Cochise, Arizona, in 1926. Among the debris of their burials, archaeologists found *metates* and *manos*, grinding stones used like a mortar and pestle. Some of the artifacts we find when excavating an archaeological site are not immediately identifiable—metates and manos are, because they are still used today and their appearance hasn't changed very much from the ones found near Cochise.

A flat palm stone and a rounded grinding stone may not seem too spectacular, but for these early people it was a discovery comparable to our splitting the atom. Now, by grinding seeds and nuts and wild grains, they had a new supply of food.

But the area was getting dryer, and less rainfall means less natural food. It wasn't an easy life for these early people. They had just discovered how to grind seeds and suddenly—in only a couple of thousand years—the seeds almost disappeared. They were hungry again.

In Europe and the Middle East, wheat is the staff of life; in the Orient, it is rice. In the Americas—corn. And these early people discovered it.

The corn of 6,000 years ago didn't look much like ours today: the ears were only a few inches long and they had no covering husks. But it was corn and since corn will grow almost anywhere under almost any climatic conditions, when these early people discovered it, they began a civilization.

Now, instead of spending all their waking hours foraging for nuts and seeds and roots—which were getting harder to find anyway—they could grow and harvest corn, eat it, and store it for the winter. Life became easier. They had time to just sit and think. They had a lot to think about, or rather, to think *up*. They went on a spree of inventing things: clothing, sandals, snaring nets, baskets, houses, jewelry, pottery, religion, a social structure—civilization.

Unrestored dwelling ruins, Ruin Park, Beef Basin Archaeological Area, Utah.

THE OLD ONES

Deep within Mancos Canyon, in southwestern Colorado, lies a stone city. It is deserted now, silent and lifeless except for the half-life it enjoys when Park Rangers and parties of tourists climb its abandoned stairways and let their voices echo within its hollow rooms. It is an empty place.

But if you listen very carefully to the wind that slices down from the Rockies and curls around the corners of this ruined city, you may hear the whispers of an ancient life—the laughter of children, the heavy tones of the tribal elders, the low murmur of woman grinding corn—the voices of the Anasazi.

The Old Ones.

Eight hundred years ago this city in Mesa Verde, and others like it scattered around the Four Corners area, were places vivid with life, centers of a healthy, bustling civilization. The people who lived in these pueblos farmed corn, raised children, worshipped their gods, grew old, died. They created pottery, wove baskets, crafted jewelry, traded with other pueblos. They laughed, sang, cried, cursed, argued, loved, hated, lived.

45

Who were the Anasazi? Where did they come from? Why, in the thirteenth century, did they abandon their great pueblos? Where did they go?

Some of these questions we may never answer; the truth of their lives is lost in the dust of the centuries. Some are slowly being answered by archaeologists who painstakingly fit small pieces into the ancient puzzle. But one question does have an answer.

Who were the Anasazi?

The Anasazi were people like anyone alive today. They had the same joys and fears, the same delights and pains that we do. They had toothaches, they killed each other, they tried to predict the weather, they believed in life after death, they gambled, and they did their best in a pretty rough world. So, look around—look at people who live each day, doing their best, accepting sorrow and hoping for happiness. These are the faces of the Anasazi.

THE BASKETMAKERS

Anasazi is a Navajo word: it means "the Old Ones." It is a mystic word, as fascinating as Aztec or Inca or Egyptian. It brings echoes of an ancient people whom we know by the magnificent ruins they left behind. But not even the Egyptians began their civilization by building the pyramids; and the Anasazi didn't start out with Mesa Verde. Before the great years of the Pueblos came the Basketmakers.

About 2,000 years ago the Basketmakers wandered into the twisted sandstone and sheer mesas of the Four Corners Country. We're not sure where they came from. Maybe they fled the burning deserts of southern Arizona, maybe they migrated from the tortured canyons of the Colorado River in Utah. Their coming wasn't a great trek of thousands of people; they came in small groups or single families. But they found the land good. There was water to grow corn and there were caves for shelter. They settled down and began a whole new chapter in the history of the Southwest.

In 1893, a cowboy-archaeologist named Richard Wetherill was riding through Butler Wash, an offshoot canyon of Grand Gulch in southern Utah. Wetherill had his share of luck: 10 years earlier he had discovered Mesa Verde. Now he found 90 bodies buried in a cave. Since the remains of these people were buried with many finely-woven baskets, Wetherill called them Basketmakers.

Thanks to the way Basketmakers were buried we have a fairly accurate picture of what they looked like. Hot, dry air and covering sand had preserved the bodies of the Basketmakers, mummifying them so well that we know that physically they were much like the modern Pueblo Indians. They were fairly short, the men averaging about 5'4" and the women about 5', muscular and stocky. Their skin was light brown and their hair was black and coarse.

We can tell a lot about them just from their hairstyle. Basketmaker men wore fairly elaborate hairdressings: long hair divided into three sections, one on each side and one in back, wound up into thick bobs and tied with string. Sometimes the hair on top was clipped extremely short except for a long queue completely wound about with cord. This could have been simple vanity but was probably a mark of rank or religious significance. The women, on the other hand, were interested in practicality. Their hair was very short, hacked off in handfuls; not overly beautiful but very useful — they used their own hair in their weaving. The men didn't seem to mind, though: Basketmaker babies kept getting born.

These early Basketmakers weren't the greatest of farmers. Their only farming implement was the digging stick — a four-foot-long stick pointed on one end — and they simply poked a hole in the ground and dropped in a seed. Corn and squash aren't very finicky, though: plant a seed, give it sun and water, and you can hardly keep it from growing. So, with some very rudimentary flood-type irrigation, the Basketmakers had a cultivated food supply that stayed in one place and was fairly reliable. Squash has an added benefit in that the hollowed-out gourds come in handy for all kinds of things. To supplement this steady food supply, the Basketmakers gathered sunflower seeds, pinon nuts, acorns, berries, roots, bulbs, grass seeds and cactus and yucca fruit.

Animal bones found at archaeological sites show that the Basketmakers caught field mice, gophers, rabbits, badgers and prairie dogs. Picking on something more their own size, the men also grabbed their spears and took off after mountain sheep, deer, cougars, even bear. They wasted nothing. Flesh was eaten, bones became ornaments or tools, hides were made into clothing, and tendons into cord.

Basketmaker spears were rather complicated affairs. Each spear had too parts. The main portion was a shaft about six feet long with a hollow drilled into each end. To the front end was fitted a hardwood shaft about six inches long tipped with a stone point. This was the business end and it was designed to break off so that if an animal was only wounded and ran off, the whole spear wouldn't disappear with the vanishing dinner. The hollow at the back end of the spear fitted over a prong on a two foot long *atlatl*, or throwing stick. The hunter would fit the spear into the *atlatl*, put his fingers into two loops attached to the middle of the *atlatl*, draw back his arm and throw. This gave his throw much more speed, force and accuracy. *Atlatl* is an Aztec word and it is really an ingenious invention, as Cortez and his soldiers discovered when they set out to conquer Mexico.

Along with spears and *atlatls*, the Basketmakers made snares and nets, some of them quite remarkable constructions. They were woven from string made of human hair and fiber of the apocynum, a milkweed-type plant, and varied from small bird-sized nets to one found at White Dog Cave, near Kayenta, Arizona, that weighed 28 pounds, was 240 feet long, 3 feet wide, and contained a whopping 4 miles of string!

HOT ROCK COOKING

Unfortunately for the Basketmakers, they were better at killing animals than killing people. The bow and arrow were used by the Hohokam and Mogollons to the south but the Basketmakers were rather slow to pick up these weapons. In Canyon del Muerto, Arizona, a tribe of Basketmakers was massacred by some wandering warrior band armed with bows and arrows. We don't know why they weren't warlike. One possibility is a religious prohibition against warfare. The Hopi say their Creation story came from their ancestors. Maybe the early Basketmakers believed in their version of Tawa and tried to live without fighting as He decreed. Whatever the reason, when they came into contact with warlike tribes, they didn't fare too well. The Basketmakers were simply peaceful farmers, not warriors.

It is a fairly accepted standard that raw food is better than no food, but cooked food is better than raw food. Meat isn't a problem. You just hack off a chunk, skewer it on a stick, and hold it over a fire — not exactly *filet mignon*, but perfectly acceptable. Corn is another thing entirely. The Basketmakers had grinding tools but raw ground corn isn't too satisfactory. However, mix it with a little water, add salt if you're lucky enough to have found a salt deposit, bake it on a hot rock, and you have a corn cake. It will keep you alive.

The Basketmakers demanded a little more from their food supply. Mix meat, corn, squash, and roots and you have a stew. There is just one problem — how to do this without any fireproof pots.

His name (or probably *her* name) has been lost for centuries but some enterprising Basketmaker cook figured out a solution. Take a basket so finely woven that it will hold water, add stewing ingredients, find a wooden scoop, pick up a hot stone from the fire and drop it into the basket. When the rock cools off, take it out and put it another. Keep doing this until the stew is cooked. You can imagine the celebration around the hearthfire that particular evening!

With the food supply stabilized and new recipes bubbling away, the Basketmakers had time to think about making themselves beautiful. Clothing wasn't their prime concern. The basic garment was a short apron, probably worn only by women, and not considered very essential even then. For protection against winter cold, not very severe in the Four Corners area, they wore animal hide blankets, or cleverly constructed blankets made from strips of rabbit fur wound around yucca fibers which were tied together in parallel rows, making a warm, lightweight blanket.

The one essential item in the Basketmaker's wardrobe was the sandal — and if you spend any time walking through the burning rocks and spiny cactus of the Four Corners country, you will quickly see why. They wove their sandals out of yucca fibers and apocynum. The sandals had thick soles and square toes and were decorated with a toe fringe of buckskin or shredded juniper bark. A cord of human hair was threaded through loops at the heel and toe and was tied around the ankle.

While their clothing wasn't exactly designed to qualify them for the Best Dressed list, their jewelry was quite elaborate. The men were particularly fond of hair ornaments, their favorite being a comb made of bone points tied together and decorated with feathers. Feathers were often tied into circles and worn as pendants. Abalone shell, proving there was a trade route to the Pacific coast, was made into necklaces. Ear pendants and necklaces were made of squash seeds and acorn cups. Some find examples of engraved bone beads and

Anasazi sandals, Canyonlands National Park collection.

polished stone beads have survived to show us that the Basketmakers appreciated beautiful things enough to spend quite a lot of time making them. It isn't easy to polish a stone when all you have to work with are other stones, sand, and deer hide.

Their love of beauty is evident in their basketry. Most baskets were made by the coil method. A coil made of small willow rods padded with yucca fibers is curled around and fastened to the coil beneath it by a thin willow splint inserted through holes made by a bone awl. This method of construction can be used for any size basket.

Most baskets were shallow trays ranging from saucer size to more than 3 feet across. Some baskets had flat bottoms with steep sides and were probably used for cooking; small baskets with small holes in the top were used for storing seeds, nuts and such. The larger water baskets and carrying baskets had pointed bottoms and flaring sides. Water baskets had small constricted openings — don't want to spill the water! — and were lined with pinyon pitch. These and carrying baskets were both shaped to fit against the shoulders and were carried on the back by means of a tump strap around the forehead of the bearer. This method leaves both hands free — extremely useful when you have to climb up or down a sheer cliff face to get to your house. For decoration, the willow sewing splints were often dyed red or black.

Another common container was a bag made by a process known as twining, in which willow rods or threads are intertwined through an upright foundation of rods or threads. The bags thus produced were soft and pliable, and varied from 3 inches to more than 2 feet in length. Usually they were made from apocynum fiber which is a warm yellowish-brown and decorated by dyeing threads red or black, making a horizontal design. Tump straps were made in the same manner. In all of these baskets, there is an artistry which goes far beyond the utilitarian.

Medicine bags were made from the skins of small animals and have been found at burial sites. Each of these consisted of two skins sewn together with the animals' heads forming the neck of the bag.

In the Basketmaker culture, corn and humans — living and dead — had pretty much the same kind of resting place. They were mostly cave dwellers — not in deep tunnel caves, but in large shallow caves weathered into the face of a sandstone cliff. When they found a likely spot close to water and good land for farming, they would level a floor in the cave and build their houses. The house floor was anywhere from 8 to 30 feet across, shaped like a saucer, and plastered with a rough flooring of adobe mud. The walls were made of sticks and small timbers lavishly plastered with adobe, and leaned inward to support the roof. Roofs were made the same way. This was extremely simple architecture but surprisingly cool in the summer and warm in the winter.

Inside the cave, sometimes inside the house, they built cists for corn storage. Cists are circular or oval holes about 2 to 4 feet deep and 3 to 8 feet in diameter. Some were divided into sections and some had adobe reinforced walls. The smaller cists were covered with slabs of sandstone, but the larger ones often had roofs of adobe and wood, and some were built with above-ground walls and roofs of timber, bark and adobe. Though cists were usually used for corn storage, some were lined with grass and used for sleeping. We're not sure why this was done but it may have had some religious significance, especially when you consider that some of the cists were used as burial chambers.

We have few details of their religion, but the Basketmakers obviously believed in some kind of afterlife, for they were buried with their personal possessions and each body was given a new pair of sturdy sandals. Dead Basketmakers were buried in a fetal position, knees drawn up to the chin, and wrapped in fur blankets, or sometimes in one of the large twined bags. A large basket usually covered the dead person's face and close at hand were weapons, digging sticks, pipes, ornaments, and more baskets—all the things he would need in his new life. The pits were lined with comfortable mattings of grass or bark and covered in the same manner as corn cists. The Basketmakers weren't quite as alone in death as we are: multiple burials were common and ranged from 2 or 3 to as many as 19. This probably indicated a tragedy of some sort, an epidemic possibly, but at least when the Basketmaker began his journey in the afterlife, he had some of his friends with him.

The frustrating part of studying burial sites is running into questions we will never be able to answer. Some of the Basketmaker graves certainly pose some of these questions. One grave in Arizona contained the body of a man wearing leather moccasins—a thing quite unknown to the Basketmakers. His body had been cut in half after death and then sewn together again. Why? Was he so different from them that they had to take a look inside to find out?

Another grave contained an 18-year-old girl and a small baby. And the entire skin from the head of another adult hung on a cord around the girl's neck. Its hair was elaborately dressed and the skin was yellow, red and white. It is possible that this is akin to the Aztec custom of a warrior wearing the flayed skin of his slain enemy, but we will never know for sure.

Perhaps the strangest of all is a grave in Canyon del Muerto. There was no body, only a pair of arms and hands. Beautiful abalone shell necklaces were wrapped around the wrists and two fine pairs of sandals lay alongside. The remains were covered by a large basket. Puzzling the significance of this burial could drive an archaeologist crazy in short order.

Burial sites are usually found near or in the settlement. Some ceremonial sites have been found far from any known dwelling place. Five Faces site in Davis Canyon and Thirteen Faces site in Horse Canyon, both in Canyonlands National Park, have been recognized as ceremonial places by the pictographs on the rock walls and grinding hollows in boulders. But what kinds of ceremonies? Possibly they were used to celebrate good hunting—the pictographs would support this

Five Faces pictographs, Davis Canyon, Canyonlands National Park, Utah.

idea—or possibly they were local versions of a pilgrimage to Mecca. In primitive societies, food gathering and religion are so closely intertwined that the ceremonial sites were probably used to celebrate both.

Whistles made of bird bones and deer hoof rattles were probably used in ceremonial dances. Pictures painted on or cut into rock faces may have some religious significance—or may just have been friendly gossip. Rock artists are discussed more fully in a later chapter of this book.

There is evidence that the Basketmakers knew the adage about "all work and no play." And it seems that they had some of the same vices we do. Gaming sticks and bones, quite similar to the ones used by today's Indians have been found—not exactly Las Vegas, but gambling implements nevertheless.

All in all, the Basketmakers were doing pretty well for themselves. They had a stable food supply, adequate housing, a religion to sustain their spirits, and time to play. Then they decided to become Modified Basketmakers.

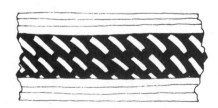

MODIFIED BASKETMAKERS

Deciding to become a Modified Basketmaker is not something you do overnight. It is a process that takes hundreds of years and, in fact, you're probably not aware you're doing it. However, by around 500 AD, most of the Anasazi were fully qualified Modified Basketmakers. As in our times, some clung to the traditional ways. Change happens at different paces in different places. Some Anasazi were a hundred years ahead of their brethren on the other side of the mountain.

The greatest difference between the Modified Basketmaker Anasazi and their ancestors was the establishment of fixed communities. The earlier Anasazi had not been particularly tied to one place. When they felt the urge to move, they moved. The Modified Basketmakers mostly decided to sit down in one place and stay there.

The villages varied in size. Some villages had only a few houses; some — obviously the Los Angeles and New York of their day — had as many as a hundred houses. Alongside the houses were granaries and, somewhere in the vicinity, a community refuse heap. Farming land and a constant water supply were nearby — only a few hundred yards away, and probably at the bottom of a sheer cliff.

Whether the village was tucked under a cliff overhang or on the flat, a new style of building emerged: the pithouse. A pithouse was a logical growth from the simple architecture of the earlier Basketmakers but much more sophisticated. And, though rudimentary by our standards, building one was not a simple matter.

The first thing to do is to dig a pit — nothing too difficult, unless the ground is hard and rocky and you don't have a shovel. But with persistence, you ended up with a pit anywhere from 3 to 5 feet deep and 9 to 25 feet in diameter. Next, the earth walls were lined with stone slabs cut by hand, or were plastered with adobe clay. Floors weren't too much of a problem — by the time this point was reached, the earth was packed flat by the workmen's feet.

The roof was a little more complicated. A typical Modified Basketmaker carpenter would heft his trusty stone axe, trot off to a likely-looking bunch of pine trees, and spend the next few days bruising eight of them until they finally gave up and fell over. Then he hacked off the branches and dragged the logs back to his pit. There he cut four of the logs so they were close to the same length and sank them upright in a square. The other four logs were laid on top and the roof framework was done. Against this framework he laid skinny poles about a foot apart braced outward to the rim of the pit, and also laid this lattice-work over the roof square.

While the Master Builder was doing the hard stuff, the wife and/or kids went rummaging around in the brush carrying back loads of twigs, bark, branches, and small bushes. These were tied onto the lattice and the whole plastered with mud reinforced with more grass and twigs. Then everyone stood back and admired their new home.

From the outside what it looked like more than anything was a big pile of dirt, but inside it was warm and weatherproof.

The early pithouses had two openings, a smokehole in the roof and a covered entry hole at one side. For some reason, they decided it was better to prop a ladder up to the roof and climb in and out the smokehole so the side entry became smaller and was left for ventilation. This may be a result of spending a lot of time on the roof anyway. Metates and manos, basket remnants, and pottery shards found on tops of roofs support this idea.

Climbing in and out of a smokehole while the fire is burning was a chancy proposition for two reasons: one, you might singe portions of your anatomy, and two, a sudden draft pulling air through the ventilation hole might set the house afire. To solve the problem of setting the house afire, an upright stone deflector slab was set between the firepit and the ventilator hole. We're not sure what they did about the problem of setting themselves afire, but since this style of architecture survived, and the Anasazi survived, we may assume that they figured something out.

Furniture was not considered a necessity. They slept on mats and squatted on the floor to eat and work, although most of the work was probably done outside. The inside of a pithouse was so dark and smoky that, except for sleeping or shelter from the weather, the people tended to live outside.

The fire pit was in the center of the house and often was the dividing line between the men's area and the women's area. On the north side, a shelf built around the wall probably served as a seating and storage area for the men. The south side of the house was separated from the north side at first by low mud walls and later by stone slabs, and it is in this area that cooking utensils and other items belonging to women's business are found. At this time, each house was its own ceremonial center and the two areas of religion and household work were probably kept apart.

The only other distinct feature of a pithouse was a hole in the floor close to the firepit which was usually kept filled with clean sand. This represented the *sipapu* hole where mankind first emerged onto the Earth. It is interesting to speculate why the *sipapu* was constructed in each house. Would someone climb out again someday? Would it someday open so that everyone could climb back in? Interesting but unprofitable speculation and we shall probably never know.

There is one thing we do know: considering the construction of the pithouse, the Modified Basketmakers must have had few enemies. A pithouse is not a fortress and there was no construction built for common defense. Life must have been fairly peaceful.

The men were learning how to build better houses and, not to be left behind, the women discovered pottery. The original idea probably came from the advanced Indian civilizations in Mexico. The Hohokam and Mogollon to the south had been making fine pottery for years, but their ideas had not drifted north to the Anasazi. Probably some Anasazi man traded for a pot and took it home to his wife. She, seeing the possibilities, set out to make more pots.

The first efforts didn't win any prizes. Plain sun-dried clay pots sagged when they got wet. Clay tempered with shredded bark and grass held together until the pot was placed over the fire, then the bark and grass burned and supper dribbled into the ashes. Finally they hit upon mixing sand with the clay and turned out some usable pots. Usable but extremely brittle.

The idea may have come from the south or they may have discovered it themselves, but the Anasazi finally found out about firing. A shaped pot was placed inside a conical pyre of wood and baked as the pyre burned itself to ashes. This method gave a characteristic white or dull gray color to the pot.

Later on, they began to decorate their pots using the same designs they had woven into their baskets: geometric lines and patterns, animal figures, and circles and dots. They painted these designs with brushes made of chewed yucca fibers. For colors, they used vegetable dyes in yellow and black, and developed a red paint which flaked off but at least imitated the redware produced by the Hohokam and Mogollon.

The Anasazi women now had a whole new range of utensils from large jugs to flat bowls, but they didn't neglect their weaving. Basket shapes didn't change much, but the designs grew richer and more elaborate. They now had pottery so, since baskets didn't have to serve every purpose, some baskets became less utilitarian and more artistic.

Sandals, especially the dress-up ones, also became more elegant, more richly decorated. The old square-toe design was replaced with a round-toe model that had black, red, and yellow designs on top and a coarse-woven sole for good traction.

With the discovery of clay pots, the women were able to utilize a new source of food: beans. It's probably that the Anasazi knew about beans before they knew about pottery but a bean is a stubborn thing. It can be ground into meal but the result isn't worth the time; it can be chewed raw but that is a good way to break your teeth—and with all the sand in their food anyway, the Anasazi had enough trouble there. Really, about the only satisfactory way to eat a bean is to boil it first—which takes forever by the hot-rock-in-a-basket-of-water method. A clay pot, however, can be left bubbling on the edge of the fire all day while you go about your business. Beans were a healthy addition to the people's low-protein diet and provided some insurance against starvation if the corn crop failed.

One high-protein food the Anasazi never took to eating was their turkeys. During this period, they domesticated both dogs and turkeys but, unlike other American Indians, they never seemed to develop a taste for either one. Dogs were probably, then as now, simply companions, but it is a little hard to figure why they bothered with turkeys. Turkeys don't sing like canaries, they are very mean-spirited birds, they get into everything, they steal food, and the end return is great piles of turkey waste on every level surface. The Anasazi used turkey feathers for blankets and decoration, but it seems simpler to go and kill one than to keep it around all the time. Possibly, considering the cantankerous nature of turkeys, they weren't so much domesticated as they just moved in and the Anasazi learned to live with them. That the Anasazi valued turkeys and dogs is proved by some graves found where the animals were buried with offerings.

Turkey petroglyph near Una Vida ruin, Chaco Canyon National Monument, New Mexico.

Possibly the Anasazi never considered turkeys as food because about this same time they discovered the bow and arrow. *Atlatls* and spears were still used, but an arrow had more range and made hunting a lot more profitable. Strangely, the Anasazi remained better at killing animals than people. There is no evidence to indicate that this new weapon led to any particular desire to puncture people instead of deer.

With hunting made easier and a two-crop economy, the Anasazi spent more time on their religion. We can't know the exact nature of their beliefs, but their ceremonial objects became richer and more elaborate. At burial sites, archaeologists have found corncobs decorated with feathers, medicine bags containing everything from corn pollen to deer antlers, polished beads and stones, and small clay figurines. The figurines seldom have arms or legs but they are clearly representations of supernatural beings.

But they weren't seriously considering the mysteries of life and death all the time. Turquoise and carved shells were now used in elegant jewelry. And they discovered music. We have found buried flutes that, after being cleaned up, can be played and produce a clear, pure tone. Such flutes were often depicted in Anasazi rock art.

The Modified Basketmakers had come a long way from their rude beginnings. They had a stable, healthy society that provided for their needs, a diverse food supply, and nice new houses to keep them warm.

Then, for some unknown reason, they got tired of living underground.

Anasazi petroglyph of legendary Kokopelli, with flute and pet dog, Chaco Canyon National Monument, New Mexico.

57

EARLY PUEBLOS

Why the Anasazi decided to move above ground is another of those unanswerable questions. We may guess—but we just don't know. And one problem with guessing, especially if you dignify that guess by calling it a theory and publish it, is that, as new evidence is found, you can look pretty silly.

One of the Classic Blunders in the archaeological guessing game happened when we began studying the Early Pueblo Anasazi. Up to this point, about 700 A.D., the Anasazi had been people with fairly long, narrow heads. Then, new excavations uncovered the remains of a people with broad, round heads. Not only were their skulls shaped differently but they used the bow and arrow, made excellent pottery, and built stone houses above ground. Obviously a new band of people, more aggressive, more civilized, had invaded the Modified Basketmakers and their advanced culture had prevailed.

Not so.

What actually happened—unless, of course, our current theory is someday proved to be another Classic Blunder—is simply that the Early Pueblo Anasazi adopted a new style of cradleboard. Up to this time, babies had been strapped into a cradleboard with a soft back. Now they started making rigid wooden cradleboards, and since an infant's skull bones are soft, any baby strapped to a hard board is going to have the back of its skull flattened while the sides bulge. Not a different race, just a new idea in skull-styling.

Why did they want deformed skulls? Possibly a few naturally broad-headed people were in positions of power here and there. Some mother may have decided that the powerful person's broad head was the reason for his success and, by gum!, her baby was going to have that advantage, too! And so a fad was born. Other mothers saw the new cradleboard and decided they, too, had to have one. (Remember the hula hoop?) Before long, mashed skulls were a new standard of beauty. This concept may sound strange until you look at our own changing standards of beauty just in the last hundred years. A curvaceous lady of the 1890s bears little resemblance to the hollow-eyed mannikins of the 1960s but both were the style of their times. On the other hand, maybe a rigid cradleboard was easier to carry than the old one. Whatever the reason, presumably the Anasazi had a good rationale for flattening their children's skulls.

Great changes were taking place throughout the Anasazi world. But not all at the same time. While the San Juan and Animas valleys in Southwestern Colorado had above-ground pueblos, in Utah's Canyonlands there lived recalcitrant *Un*modified Basketmakers. Some villages had pithouses and pueblos together in the same way that some modern Americans live in Buckminster Fuller domes, some in brick houses, and some in log cabins. Strangest of all, in Davis Canyon, in Canyonlands National Park, among all the stone structures of the Anasazi stands a log cabin. Who built that one?

When they moved above ground, they started to build *jacal* houses. The early *jacal* houses were built of poles and plastered with adobe; the first ones had sloping walls and were constructed over a shallow pit. As time passed, the walls became perpendicular and the pit disappeared. Some enterprising builder decided to use sandstone slabs to reinforce his adobe walls and the idea caught on. Before long, shaped stone was the principal building material. Since the walls were now straight up and down, people began joining houses together — that way you only have to build three walls. And so the unit house came into existence.

Unit houses had flat roofs and no doors on the ground floor. All entries were made through holes in the roofs and if you were *avant-garde* enough to live in one of the newfangled two-story houses, and if you lived on the ground floor, you had to climb down through your upstairs neighbor's apartment to reach your own. This didn't seem to bother anyone, though: the Anasazi lived a friendly, communal life with very little of our sense of privacy.

Unit houses were no more built for defense than were pit houses. The unit was built in a straight line or a slight crescent. Sometimes there was only a single row, sometimes a double row, and even though ladders could be pulled up to the roof, a determined enemy could have breached their flimsy defenses in no time. At this stage, villages usually contained thirty houses or less per unit so they would have been easy pickings for warrior tribes like the Ute and Shoshone who came later. But for now, their life was peaceful.

As their worldly life moved to the top of the ground, their ceremonial life went deeper into the earth. Their houses were reaching in new directions, but the religious ways of their ancestors were probably not to be tampered with. We do the same in our culture: compare St. Patrick's Cathedral to the U.N. Building in New York City. The pithouse deepened to become a *kiva.*

Kiva is a modern Indian word, but modern *kivas* are built almost identical to Anasazi *kivas* so we may assume that more than just the architecture stayed the same. Religions are not as subject to change as are mundane customs.

Kivas were built entirely underground. From topside the only way to find one was to look for a flat, stone-paved circle with a hole and a ladder. The old pithouse features were retained. Each *kiva,* then and now, had a firepit, a deflector slab, and a *sipapu* hole. A two- or three-foot high stone-lined bench encircled the walls and was broken by six or eight masonry columns that supported the roof. The roof itself, made of logs, was thick enough to stand the weight of stone, and people walking over the top.

Modern Pueblo Indians are probably direct cultural descendants of the Anasazi, so we may take a chance and guess at the uses of the Anasazi *kiva.*

The *kiva* was both a religious center and a social club—for men only. A village might have several *kivas:* one for each men's society. A man's social club had two purposes, the first being religious: each society had some area of expertise in influencing the gods, some special skill in appeasement that must be performed for the good of the village. The second was socio-cultural: to induct young men into the ways of manhood and to get away from the women.

Women held a lot of power in Anasazi life. Descent was through the female line and when a man married, he moved in with his wife's family. She owned the home and important decisions were made by

Detail of partially restored Great Kiva at Casa Rinconada ruin in Chaco Canyon National Monument, New Mexico.

her family. If she got entirely fed up with him, she could throw him out of the house, bag and baggage. Male children were taught by the mother's male relatives. Small wonder that the men wanted a place all their own. In the *kivas*, he could take care of his religious duties, retreat from his mother-in-law, and grumble with the other men about nagging wives. Women were allowed in *kivas* only on special ceremonial occasions.

The *kiva* was not the only ceremonial center. We have found large circles paved in adobe and enclosed with upright stone slabs. These are believed to be dance courts. The light of Tawa's sun may have shone down on stamping feet and swaying bodies as the Anasazi danced their supplications to supernatural powers.

While the men were supplicating or grumbling in their *kivas*, the women were discovering thermodynamics. Up to this time, pottery was smoothly shaped, inside and out. Now they began to make cooking pots with corrugated surfaces. This was done simply by not smoothing out the dimples where the coils of clay had been pinched together. The heat transference from a corrugated surface to the smooth inside of a pot made boiling beans a lot faster — which comes in handy at 5000' elevations.

Pottery designs, colors, and shapes became more diversified. Handles were added and some of the shapes became so fanciful that today we haven't a clue as to their use. Black-on-white was still the principal color scheme, but in the Alkali Ridge area of Southeastern Utah, the women decided to decorate their pottery with red designs on a pink-orange background. The idea never caught on in other areas.

Unfortunately, as their potting skills increased, Anasazi basketry went sadly downhill, probably a natural consequence of their interest in pottery. The large flat baskets so beautifully woven and characteristic of their ancestors almost disappeared. Sandals were still tough and utilitarian but the artistic decorations faded away.

Somewhere about this time, some roving Anasazi trader brought back a strange piece of cloth. It was soft and smooth, it wasn't fur and it wasn't yucca fibers. Since it was not as durable, not many pieces have survived, but durability isn't necessarily as important as is newness. What was this new cloth? Cotton. The Hohokam had discovered cotton some years before and now it had worked its way north. We're not sure when the Anasazi learned to grow, spin, and weave their own cotton, but they began to wear it.

We know about cotton cloth and basketry and pottery because each village had its refuse heap. All the material things of Anasaki life, when they were broken or used up, ended on the trash heap. Including people.

The dead weren't just thrown away like broken pottery, but in a hard, rocky land, you dig graves in the easiest place. There is evidence that some of the dead were cremated; some remains were sealed up in abandoned houses or storage pits; and sometimes babies were buried under the floors of their houses near the firepit, kept near their mothers. That, more than possibly anything else, tells us how the Anasazi loved their families.

If, a couple of thousand years from now, some archaeologist digs in our cemeteries, he won't know very much about us. We send nothing with our dead, not pottery, not their favorite dogs, not good sturdy sandals. That archaeologist may deduce that we don't believe in an afterlife, since we don't physically prepare our dead to live again.

Not so with Anasazi trash heap burials. Pit burials with all their accouterments tell us what they believed about the next world. The trash heap burials tell us a lot about how they lived in this world. Pottery, sandals, baskets, clothing — these are all tangible evidences of Anasazi life. But from the burials, we also learn about their intangible life.

Some primitive societies abandon people who are not productive members of the group. When we find the remains of an old woman so badly crippled she couldn't possibly have cared for herself, we know that the Anasazi valued people for more than their physical usefulness.

Unlike later Indian societies, inbreeding was allowed. Three skeletons found at one site had fused ribs. This is an unusual phenomenon resulting from marrying and having children too close to your own bloodline.

Burials near southeastern Utah show that the people suffered from vitamin deficiencies and malnutrition. This more northern center had problems with its neighbors. Two men died from blows to the head and one had been shot with an arrow and scalped. Many skeletons of children all buried at the same time indicate an epidemic of some sort.

But, as always in the archaeological puzzle, for each question answered, a hundred more remain unanswered. In many villages, there simply aren't enough burials to account for the population. What happened to the rest of the people? In some graves, we have found only a skull, no body. Maybe this was because if a man was killed far from home, it was easier to just carry back his head for burial. But what about skeletons buried with no heads? The guessing game is wide open.

We do know that by 1000 A.D., the Anasazi had settled into a stable pattern. Villages were made of rectangular unit houses, underground *kivas*, a trash heap at one end, and fields nearby. This pattern would never change substantially. The pueblos would get bigger, the population would increase, but the Anasazi were now established in the lifestyle that would continue as long as they did.

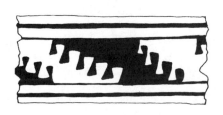

THE GREAT YEARS

For a thousand years, from early Basketmakers to early Puebloans, the Anasazi were a tiny people, scrabbling an existence from a hard land. They borrowed the innovations in their culture from others like the Hohokam and Mogollon. But they were inquisitive, hard-working and adaptable. Now they became the guiding force rather than the borrowers.

The heart of Anasazi culture was around the Four Corners area, but what they created was so powerful that people as far away as Big Bend, Texas imitated their ideas, and across the Colorado River in Utah, Anasazi ideas penetrated the Fremont culture to the north. The spreading Anasazi culture created the golden age of Southwestern prehistory.

They built to last. Today, thousands of people visit Mesa Verde in Colorado, Aztec and Chaco Canyon in New Mexico, and Betatakin and Canyon de Chelly in Arizona. Hovenweep National Monument is the principal site in Utah, but visitors to Canyonlands who like to hike and investigate hidden places may find tucked under a cliff overhang a wall of stone, a house with a broken pot, a place where the Anasazi lived. Their influence on Southwestern life is indelible.

Up to this time, the Anasazi had lived in villages totaling no more than a few hundred people, and most settlements had far fewer. Now they began to congregate, answering some call that is a mystery to us. They were certainly a gregarious people and their villages became cities. Their houses became "apartment houses" — Pueblo Bonito in

Canyon-rim Anasazi ruin, Hovenweep National Monument, Utah.

Chaco Canyon National Monument is a single building complex and could house 1200 people. It was the largest "apartment house" in the entire world for 600 years.

The change in architecture caused more differences in their lives than just more ladders to climb. When the Anasazi lived in scattered villages, government was taken care of by the head of the clan. Each man had to know all the skills of living, from the pragmatics of farming to the best methods of divine supplication. This changed with the building of the massive pueblos.

Some of these cities had as many as 6,000 people. With all those people living together, centralized government became necessary. The particulars elude us, but based on the organization of modern Pueblo Indians, government must have been fairly democratic. Absolute rulers have better housing than the hoi polloi, and they tend to build statues of themselves on every corner. There is no evidence of this among the Anasazi.

The enormous construction tasks they undertook required communal labor. The Anasazi understood the benefits of sacrifice for the common good. Among themselves, they were a peaceful, cooperative, hardworking people.

When so many people live together, one man is going to be better at a particular skill than the man next door, and thus specialization is born. A man who makes fine arrowheads may concentrate on his trade and, when he needs a new pot to boil beans, will offer an arrowhead or two to the woman up the street who makes superb pots. A woman who makes superb pots talks to another woman who is a fine potter and, as they share ideas, they both end up making even better pots. Cooperation stimulates ideas and creates more leisure time. With more leisure time, art and religion advance. With artistic and religious development, life becomes more elaborate, more satisfying, more civilized.

Why did they decide to group together? Again, the answer is lost in the sands of the centuries. The large pueblos, particularly in a place like Chaco Canyon, were quite defensible. They could simply pull up their ladders and wait. Common defense may have been a factor. But they didn't build hastily. They took their time and changed things a lot. Defense building is usually speedy building.

Why did they keep changing things around? They were continually building and tearing down walls, moving rooms, destroying old storage rooms and building over them. One theory is that their life was so cooperative, structured and peaceful that they needed an outlet for all that repressed energy. One wonders what theorists would make of our building new homes and moving from one house to another in the same town. Perhaps the Anasazi were just like us and got tired of looking at the same old walls.

When the men took time from their building and farming, they invaded the women's province and sat down at their looms. Though women had perfected weaving techniques long ago, the men decided

64

that cotton needed a man's touch. Their looms were kept in the *kivas* and, considering that people are people, several men weaving probably bore a distinct resemblance to a modern quilting bee. They wove blankets, breechclouts and ponchos; their garments were draped or tied. They never hit on the idea of tailored clothing.

With the increasing use of cotton, human hair was not so necessary for weaving, so the women let their hair grow, twisting it into great knobs over their ears. Those ears—and the necks and arms of both men and women—were decorated with some of the most beautiful jewelry ever designed. Shell beads were strung for earrings or carved into pendants shaped like birds and animals. They started using the sky stone: rough nuggets of turquoise appeared as earrings or were smoothed and shaped into beads or carved into frogs and birds. A necklace from Pueblo Bonito was made of 2,500 beads and four polished pendants. With our modern lapidary tools how can we begin to appreciate the labor and love that went into the creation of that necklace?

Another of their ornaments raises interesting questions. They wore small copper bells, yet they had no knowledge of working copper. The only reasonable source of those bells was the Indian civilizations of Mexico. It is 2,000 miles from the Four Corners to Mexico City. Who made that journey? Who carried those copper bells on foot through some of the harshest country on this planet? The persistence of human beings in obtaining their desires is truly remarkable.

Robes and blankets were made from turkey and parrot feathers. And the parrot feathers also came from Mexico.

Nor was pottery neglected—

Now, wait a minute. Pottery again? Why all this emphasis on pottery? A pot is a pot, right? Yes—and no. Most of the tangible objects of any civilization deteriorate with time—that's why we have so few pieces of Anasazi cotton cloth. But pottery, whole or broken, is nearly indestructible. A potsherd can lie buried for thousands of years and when it is dug up, still tell us much about the people who made it. The fact that some of the older Anasazi pots found bear Hohokam designs indicates that there was a trade route. When a piece of thin-rimmed Chaco Canyon pottery appears among the chunky vessels of Mesa Verde, we know someone made the trip. Someone who visited Mesa Verde and left that pot took his ideas back with him to Chaco. So pottery is just as important to the archaeologist as his magnifying glass was to Sherlock Holmes.

Cliff Palace ruin, Mesa Verde National Park, Colorado.

Kin Kletso ruin, Chaco Canyon National Monument, New Mexico.

The Anasazi built two different types of pueblos. One style was the cliff dwelling, best illustrated at Mesa Verde and Betatakin. The other was the apartment house constructed on flat-land places such as Chaco Canyon.

Mesa Verde lies in southwest Colorado between the towns of Durango and Cortez. On Chapin Mesa lies the whole history of the Anasazi, from pit house to pueblo to cliff dwelling.

Cliff Palace within Mesa Verde National Park, was built around 1200 A.D. The masonry style used in this cliff dwelling isn't nearly as fine as at some other places; in fact, when Cliff Palace was built, the Anasazi culture had started to decline. But nowhere else does the ancient mystery and splendor of the Anasazi reach out to us as at Cliff Palace. It is a sky castle, a place of sunlight on golden stone slashed with dark shadows.

For a hundred years before the building of Cliff Palace, the Anasazi's peaceful way of life was breaking up. Warrior tribes were invading the farmers of Mesa Verde. Many villages were abandoned and the people grouped into pueblos built with massive double walls and high towers. *Kivas* were moved inside the structure for protection. Farmlands too far from the pueblos were relinquished to the wilderness again. With less farmland, the population declined. But whoever was raiding the villages was too powerful so, as a last resort, the Anasazi left the comforts of the mesa top and moved into the caves under the mesa rim. Cliff Palace was the last flowering of a doomed civilization — but it was magnificent.

The caves which house Cliff Palace and the other cliff dwellings of Mesa Verde and Canyon de Chelly aren't the shallow caves used by the Basketmakers. They are huge vaults under overhangs of stone, protected from rain and snow but open to the sun. The only access to the caves are small trails easy to defend, or toe-holds cut into the cliff itself. Some of the caves housed hundreds of people, some only tens or just a single family, but they are all fortresses, almost impossible to attack.

Water and farmland, however, couldn't be moved to the caves. Very few caves had water sources in them; usually the women had to balance their pitchers, climb a hundred feet up or down the cliff, and carry the water back. Farming had to be done under the watchful eyes of sentries and each farmer kept his weapons close to hand. Enemies were closing in on the Anasazi and the only place they were safe was in their cliff houses. This is a physically hard life but for a people as inherently peaceful as the Anasazi, psychologically it was an even harder way of life.

Cliff Palace is one of the largest cliff dwellings, with *kivas* and more than 200 rooms. Some of its buildings are four stories high, the walls braced against the top and sides of the cave. Its rooms are small, averaging only 6 feet by 8 feet with ceilings only 4 or 5 feet high. Windows are tiny and doorways only 2 feet high and 16 inches wide. This leads us to wonder if the Anasazi were small people. They weren't. The men averaged about 5'4", which is about the same as the standard European of 1200 A.D., but house size was dictated by the boundaries of the cave. The small doorways, built in a T-shape, were less drafty and easier to defend. The people spent very little time in these cramped, dark rooms but even then they took time to plaster the walls and paint designs and murals in yellow, red, black and white.

Most of the waking life was spent either in the fields and hunting, or in the open plaza on the cave floor. There, the women ground corn and made pottery, the men chipped arrows and made deerhide medicine bags, and the children played and chased turkeys. For 100 years these cliffs and canyons echoed with voices of Anasazi life. Now the doorways are empty, and lifeless windows stare silently at the tourists who visit Cliff Palace.

The cliff dwellings, hauntingly beautiful as they are, do not represent the finest flowering of Anasazi culture. That award may be claimed by the people of Chaco Canyon in northwestern New Mexico. There, on a mile-wide plain, lie the ruins of a city that, at one time, was home for 6,000 people. A little before 950 A.D. while most of the Anasazi were struggling with the intracacies of building *jacal* houses and some were trotting north to become Fremonts, the people of Chaco Canyon embarked on the greatest building project in North America. Before they were done, they had constructed 12 large pueblos and more than 400 smaller ones. The most spectacular single ruin is the Beautiful Village, "Pueblo Bonito."

The first walls of Pueblo Bonito were made of sandstone slabs roughly hewn and mortared with adobe and rock chips. They were pretty sloppy work, as if the builders weren't exactly sure of what they were doing. About 100 years later some Anasazi from the north moved in. They were better builders, who started with a core of adobe and rubble, then faced it with squared-off sandstone blocks using much less mortar. Learning as they built, after not too many years they were using sandstone blocks about 3 inches thick alternating with blocks 1 inch thick. By the time they quit building, their walls were constructed of uniform sandstone blocks that would do credit to any stonemason, before or since.

Like other pueblos, Pueblo Bonito was changed and rebuilt, walls were moved, sections torn down and replaced, but when they finally deserted the place, Pueblo Bonito covered more than three acres, rose to 5 stories high in some places, and had over 800 rooms.

To the modern eye, there seem to be as many *kivas* as there are rooms. They didn't dig their *kivas* into the ground but built walls, roofed them over, and filled in the spaces with more apartments and rubble so the underground effect was maintained. In addition to all the 25-foot-diameter *kivas* there are several *Great Kivas*, 60 feet in diameter, that served as sacred places for the whole community. A reconstructed *kiva* of this sort is open to visitors in the ruins at Aztec, New Mexico.

Each family had a living room and a storage room, but they still

West end of Pueblo Bonito ruin, Chaco Canyon National Monument, New Mexico. The ruin has been partially restored, and stabilized for public visitation.

had to clamber up ladders and through their neighbors' rooms to reach their own. Cooking was done on the roofs and in the plazas, as were all other activities of mundane daily life. Pueblo Bonito wasn't different from other pueblos, just much larger.

In the latter years of Pueblo Bonito, the doors and windows in the outside wall were sealed up. The gateway into the pueblo was narrowed several times, then blocked off completely. The only way into the pueblo was via ladders — their enemies were getting bolder.

Cliff Palace and Pueblo Bonito are the classics of Anasazi life. But the Old Ones' presence echoes in all corners of the high desert from Keet Seel and Betatakin in northern Arizona to Edge of the Cedars and Hovenweep near Blanding, Utah, and Horse and Salt Creek Canyons in Canyonlands National Park. They created a civilization unequaled in North America, grand cities in some respects rivaling the Toltecs and Maya in Mexico. Then they disappeared.

CULTURAL DECLINE

Why did the Anasazi abandon their fields and glorious pueblos? Why did they leave the places they had lived for centuries? What happened?

There is no single answer to these questions. In fact, we're not sure of any answers. But there are several theories and from these we may build an explanation.

In the latter part of the 13th century, Anasazi-land experienced almost 20 years of drought. In a land that is a desert to begin with, drought was a heartbreaking thing. Corn shriveled in the field, squash vines dried up before the tiny squash nubbins formed. Bean plants withered. Near artesian wells, some water could be transported to the crops, but they must have had to rely increasingly on hunting and stored supplies. But when the water left, so did the game animals.

What little rain that did fall was quickly lost. The Anasazi

Mesa Verde Jug

contributed to their downfall by committing ecological suicide. They had lived through periods of drought before because under the worst conditions, even the high desert holds a little moisture in the soil. The infrequent rains were trapped in potholes and in the ground cover itself. But the Anasazi used timber to roof their buildings. They stripped the hillsides and mesa-tops of trees, leaving no root systems to check the water runoff. When the rains came, they sliced deep arroyos and cut through the fields carrying away the fertile soil. Flood plain irrigation died, since the water rushing down the valleys cut deep channels instead of spreading out. The grasses and bushes that lived beyond the fields died and when that cover was gone, the runoff was even worse. Year by year their fields grew smaller and poorer.

With a decreasing food supply, their resistance to disease

Large utility jar, Canyonlands National Park collection.

lessened. Malnourished people die very quickly and the children usually die first. Communicable diseases ravished the weakened Anasazi settlements.

Each pueblo was composed of several clans. As they grew hungry and their children died, the clans began to look at each other with suspicion. When hard times come, you protect your own. The easy communal life began to break up.

At the same time the Anasazi were fighting for survival against the natural world, the Shoshonean raiders moved into their land. For a couple of hundred years the pueblos had been growing more like fortresses. Now these warlike nomads came in increasing numbers. They suffered from the bad hunting because of the drought, the same as the Anasazi, and the great pueblos with their stored food supplies were tempting prizes.

Once a pueblo pulled up its ladders and men with weapons bristled the walls, the raiders were stymied. They couldn't take the place by force and the defenders were better able to stand a siege than the besiegers. But they could raid the fields, stealing ripened crops and burning the rest while the villagers helplessly watched. A few years of this kind of hopeless struggle could drive anyone from his land. Food was increasingly hard to grow, and then, after all that back-breaking labor, to have it stolen or destroyed and spend the winter watching your children die — they gave up.

There was no mass exodus. They left a few at a time, a surviving family here, a clan there. But in less than a hundred years they were gone. Some moved into places others had left and continued the struggle for a few more years. Others tried to rebuild their lives in the same style — the pueblo at Aztec was probably built by refugees from Chaco Canyon. But after a generation, they moved on.

When the Mesa Verde people abandoned their cliff houses, they wandered south and found the deserted pueblo at Aztec. They moved in and rebuilt some of it to their preference. In less than 100 years, they, too, deserted the pueblo.

In moving south, they came up against other settled cultures, such as the Hohokam, in central Arizona. The Hohokam didn't seem to mind this invasion of farmers and the different cultures began to mesh.

The modern Hopi Indians consider themselves to be direct descendants of the Old Ones and many of their cultural determinants support this claim.

Acoma, a modern Zuni pueblo located about 60 miles west of Albuquerque, was settled about 1300 by Mesa Verde wanderers.

The Anasazi spread all over the Southwest during their great migration. Their culture mixed with others and changed, but they were the determining influence until the Spaniards arrived in the mid-1500s. Their faces can still be seen in the pueblos of modern Southwest Indian tribes. Their ruins stand as mute and desolate sentinels of a grandeur that has seldom been equalled and will never be seen again.

The Fremont Culture

Fremont petroglyphs, Fremont River gorge, Capitol Reef National Park, Utah.

ORIGINS

The prehistoric Fremont Indians of Utah left no great ruins like the Anasazi. They were not mathematicians or astronomers like the Maya. In fact, most modern Americans have never heard of them, but the remains of their occupancy have sparked off one of the greatest controversies in southwestern archaeology: where did the Fremont come from? It is the kind of question that disrupts sedate archaeological conferences as researchers man the barricades of their favorite theories. The problem is one that may be solved as more discoveries are made, but right now, no one theory is definitive.

While there are several different theories, each one with its own plausibility, most researchers support one of three basic positions, two of which may some day prove to be Classic Blunders, while the proponents of the other one may chortle and say, "See, we were right."

One of the basic theories is that the Fremont were a group of Anasazi who split off and headed north, taking their Basketmaker culture with them. Many of the Fremont culture indicators appeared in the Anasazi civilization at the right period to support this theory. One of the problems here is that, in many ways, the Fremont were quite different from their Anasazi neighbors, i.e., they made leather

73

moccasins, used an entirely different kind of mano and metate, never clustered in large cities, and seemed to be much more warlike.

Another basic theory is that the Fremont, like the Anasazi, developed from an older Desert Archaic culture and simply borrowed some Anasazi ideas. This means that they were a hunting and gathering people who accepted the traits of a more advanced civilization, just as the Anasazi, Hohokam and Mogollon accepted the ideas coming up from Mexico. One of the problems with this theory is that there is an archaeological hiatus of around 2000 years between remains of the Desert Archaic culture and the first remains dated as Fremont.

The third generally reputable theory is that the Fremont were originally hunters and gatherers from the high western plains who moved into Utah at some unspecified time. This theory is supported by some evidence that they were a slightly different physical type from their southern neighbors, but this has not been proved to the satisfaction of researchers because of the paucity of skeletons recovered. In the great dispersal that took place around 1250 A.D., the Fremont probably became the nomadic Ute-Shoshonean peoples. This, too, is a difference from the Anasazi. While this theory has some plausibility, there is simply not enough evidence to support it at this time.

While none of the theories is unassailable, the fact remains that by 400 A.D., there were people living in Utah, and archaeologists now classify them as Fremonts.

THE LAND

Unless you can find beauty in the twisted sandstone and sere plateaus of the high desert, it may be hard to understand why people would choose to live in the land the Fremont chose.

They ranged over almost all of what is now the State of Utah, excepting only the extreme southern part and southeast beyond the Colorado River. Some of their land was mountainous, white-capped peaks that were still glaciated when the Fremont knew them. But most of the people lived in the lowlands between 4000' and 8000' elevation.

Despite their proximity to glaciated mountains, and to rivers such as the Colorado, Green, Sevier, Dirty Devil and Fremont, the Fremont Indians lived in a land where water, or the lack of it, dictated how people lived. Annual precipitation in the Fremont lands today averages 10 inches per year. It is probable that 1000 years ago that figure was a little higher but, in comparison, the Midwest state of Indiana averages about 30 inches per year. Thus, the Fremont were essentially a desert people.

The land is bare rock and sand. Except in river bottoms and along creeks, there is very little soil; but if you can get water to the land, it will produce some crops.

In the creek bottoms grow cottonwoods, willow, tamarisk, mosses and delicate-leaved desert flowers. Away from the creeks, the desert is dominated by less friendly vegetation such as greasewood, saltbush, cacti, and yucca. On the mesas, juniper and pinyon pine scrabble their roots into cracks in the rocks; the mountain foothills are clothed in aspen and ponderosa pine.

It is a harsh, ungentle land to call home, but for almost 1000 years, the Fremont survived in it.

THE PEOPLE

It is doubtful that there were ever more than 10,000 Fremonts at any one time, if that many. Some sites archaeologists have discovered may have had 200 or 300 residents, but mostly they lived in small groups.

One good reason for small population centers is the difficulty of finding or growing food in an arid land. Like all primitive societies, much of their food supply depended on what plants they could find. Their diet consisted heavily of juniper seeds, wild lily bulbs, greasefoot seeds, and pinyon nuts.

The Fremont, like their Anasazi neighbors, made snares and nets that enabled them to catch rabbits, prairie dogs, ground squirrels, chipmunks and gophers.

Some enterprising Fremont hunter must have grown tired of nuts and meat because at the Mantle Cave site researchers found fishhooks. The hooks are barbs of carved bone fastened to a wooden shaft. Not much like the array of flies, plugs, and spinners found in a modern sporting goods store, but they must have worked—fish bones were found beside them.

The traditional Fremont hunter used a bow and arrow but, strangely, there is no evidence they used spears. We have found arrowheads and chipped stone knives, but nothing that can definitely be identified as a spearhead.

Our meat supply, excluding chickens and such, is fairly limited to beef, pork and sheep. The Fremont hunted bighorn sheep, deer, elk, bear, grouse, beaver, badger, coyote, wolves and buffalo. They caught mice, rabbits, skunks and insects. Grasshoppers were trapped, ground up and stored in pits—"a little grasshopper salt on your elk meat, dear?" Which of these animals they ate and which they used for clothing and implements we're not sure, but they had the whole world as their supermarket and department store.

Hunting and gathering are fine but, remember, leisure time is necessary to develop art, religion and other aspects of civilization. And leisure time is next to impossible to find without a stable food supply. Since they built fairly permanent villages, and since these villages are almost always close to irrigatable land, agriculture must have played a large part in their lives.

Farmer Fremont got up with first light in the morning, yawned, stretched, and, gathering up his digging stick and shovel, headed for his field. He studied the sky for a hint of rain and was usually disappointed. Instead of thunderheads, all he saw was the huge brazen blue desert sky with maybe a pale wisp of cloud lying along the horizon.

He planted in much the same manner as the Mesa Verde Anasazi. Poke a hole with a digging stick or make a furrow, drop in a seed, and cover it up. His shovel bears a close resemblance to a modern hoe and was probably used in the same way. His agricultural efforts weren't too complicated but, like any good farmer, he grew crops fitted to the land: corn, beans and squash.

Where Farmer Fremont excelled was in his irrigation system. If his field was situated in a run-off area or if it rained, he could rest in the shade of a rock and watch while a flood of water a foot deep and a hundred yards wide watered his crops for him. But despite the fact that the mountains in his land were still glaciated and glacier melt added to the spring run-off, that didn't happen very often.

Early white settlers in the Fremont area discovered ditches leading from water sources to the flatlands. Some of these ditches were several miles long. Imagine digging a five-mile ditch through rocky desert soil with a wooden shovel. And not one, but many. When Farmer Fremont set out to grow a crop, he may have prayed for a little Divine help but he put his back into it, too. With a little reconstruction, some of his irrigation ditches are still being used by farmers today.

After Farmer Fremont put that much effort into growing a crop, he wasn't about to let anything happen to it after the harvest. With so much work already invested, he didn't want it stolen by rodents, insects or strangers.

If you have a good eye and spend some time looking, you can find granaries all over Fremont land. Most of these are small structures made of rock and adobe tucked under rock shelters, or along slips on a cliff. Most are camouflaged or practically inaccessible. They were built with care and carefully repaired. Openings were large enough only for an arm and give evidence of having been sealed. Not even an insect could get inside.

Some granaries are located close to village sites, some close to fields, and some don't seem to be close to anywhere at all. Proximity to a village or a field is easily explained on the basis of convenience. What about the ones that were not close to either place? Were they for the storage of wild foods gathered in that vicinity? Did a village once exist there, with all traces of it long since obliterated, either by weather or unfriendly neighbors? Possibly the Fremont dispersed their food in small caches so if one were destroyed, they wouldn't go hungry. They may have moved the village and not moved the granary, either on purpose or by accident. Have you ever moved and left a box in the old house? Some of the small caches may simply have been forgotten.

Typical cliff-ledge granary of the type constructed by both Anasazi and Fremont prehistoric indians.

77

Inside the village, each house usually had its small storage room attached. Sometimes several of these storage rooms would be connected and made a structure all their own.

The Fremont seem to have been more aggressive than their southern neighbors, and so they built squat towers in places difficult to get to. These were probably used for communal food storage. If you were farming better fields than your neighbors two valleys away, and if these neighbors took to hungrily eyeing your crops, you might consider it a good idea to put the bulk of your harvest in one place that could be defended. For the Fremont, losing a crop didn't mean taking out a loan at the bank for next year—it meant some of them were going to die.

The towers were built on top of a hill or in a canyon with only one twisted trail leading in or out. They could be defended by just a few determined men. In many places, close to the towers, they built small, crumbly stone houses to shelter the guards. We may extrapolate that guard duty was held on a rotating basis, each able man in the village taking his turn. Maybe the Fremont invented the military draft in North America.

If you grow a crop, harvest a crop, and successfully defend a crop, the next step is to eat that crop. Fremont culinary efforts weren't too elaborate. They, like all the Southwest farming Indians, ground corn with mano and metate so they had corn cakes and cornmeal mush. Their metate was different from the Anasazi model. It had a trough at one end and is one of the purely Fremont designs. Meat was roasted over the fire and, since they discovered pottery about the same time as the Anasazi, beans were boiled and stews made with recipes handed down from their grandmothers.

We're not certain but they may have liked popcorn. Charred baskets were probably used for popping or parching seeds and corn.

They may have been the originators of the crock pot. They chipped holes in flat rock formations, some large enough to hold five gallons of liquid. Many of these large holes have small holes surrounding them, looking more than anything like a pot surrounded by condiment trays. We can't be certain what the holes were used for, but they aren't situated to catch water runoff so it is not too unreasonable to assume that they were improvements on the hot-rock-in-a-basket style of cooking. This area, however, is wide open for guesses. Since they had pottery vessels for cooking, the rock holes may have had a different use entirely.

And after a solemn feast, there's nothing like a good smoke. They made pipes from both pottery and stone, some of them finely decorated. As with their descendants, pipes were probably sacred things used in worshipping the spirits rather than just an after-dinner smoke. Since very little tobacco grows in the desert, it's interesting to speculate on what they smoked.

While the Fremont may at one time have been Basketmaker Anasazi, by the time they moved north basketry had already begun to decline in favor of pottery. They made fewer baskets than the Anasazi and in fewer different styles, but a wider range of materials went into their construction. The most common technique was the coiling method used by the Anasazi. Coiled baskets were usually shallow bowls made of willow, yucca or squawbush. Very seldom did these baskets have any decoration. They used cedar bark and grass for some larger baskets and one sample, a water bottle, was waterproofed with pitch. From the lack of craftsmanship and the few examples found, Fremont women just didn't spend much of their time making baskets.

Pottery is another story altogether. Because of their firing methods, all Fremont pottery is gray. Other than that, one Fremont pot seldom looked like any other Fremont pot. They made fat-bellied jars, flat bowls, upright bowls, tight-mouthed jars, tall pitchers, short pitchers, jars with flaring rims, jars with recurved rims, jars with handles, jars with lids, pots shaped like animal heads and pots with serpent handles.

Almost all of their pots were smooth. Very few examples of corrugated ware have been found and those may have been items of trade. But they didn't often leave them smooth. In fact, the most distinctive feature of Fremont pottery is its decoration. A Fremont woman must have been offended by a smooth pot for as soon as she had her basic shape, she started changing it. A strip of clay might be wound around the rim or several clay pellets stuck onto the shoulders; a handle might be shaped like a rattlesnake. She used flint chips, twigs or her fingernails to tool a decorative band around her pot. When the pot was fired and cool, she got out her paint brush. She made paint from charcoal and iron ore and plants. She painted bands and dots and whorls, geometric designs and figures from the land around her. Sometimes, before a particularly complicated decorating job, she would cover the pot with whitewash to give her painting a brighter background.

After all that effort, when a pot broke, a Fremont lady wasn't about to throw it away. Broken pieces with enough curve were used to hold her paints for the next pot. Some shards were used as scrapers for hides or other pottery; some were reworked into beads and pendants; some were shaped into circles and used as spindle whorls, although the men may have confiscated a few of these to use in their gambling games. Mrs. Fremont knew about "Waste not, want not."

Their love of diversity was also evident in their architecture. In contrast to the Anasazi, who were conformists, each Fremont seemed to delight in being different from his neighbors. In the same village, *jacal* houses, unit houses and pithouses can be found. Houses were built in the open, under rock overhangs, above ground and below it. They used dry-stone construction, upright sandstone slabs, stone mortared with adobe, poles plastered with mud, and roofed-over plaster-lined pits. Sometimes their rooms were round and sometimes they were rectangular. If a man wanted to build a house in a certain place, and that place already had a boulder too heavy to move, he simply made that boulder part of one wall and built around it. One man paved his floor with stone slabs; his neighbor plastered his with adobe; the fellow on the other side of the rock decided hard-packed dirt was good enough for him. What his wife thought may have been another matter. This crazy quilt pattern of building had none of the uniform balanced arrangement so loved by the Anasazi, but it infers a less rigid people, less bound by restricting tradition.

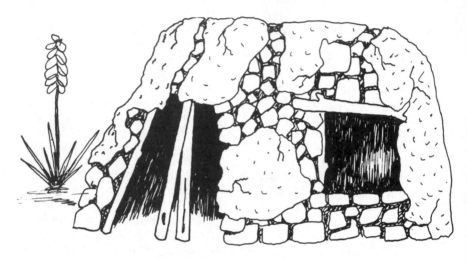

FREMONT HOUSE

When they left their villages to hunt or trade, they had a well-developed network of "motels." All over Fremont land you can find small rock shelters. Not the kind of place where people lived, but shelter from the elements on overnight stops. Some of the small food caches may have been wayside "restaurants."

They had their ceremonial places, the same as the Anasazi. The Fremont didn't go underground to worship their gods. They built no *kivas*. But on high places, if you look carefully you may see where the ground has been leveled and packed smooth by dancing feet. If you are very lucky, you may find the remnants of a rock wall or standing monoliths put there for the glory of the gods. The monoliths aren't Stonehenge—the Fremont didn't build that big—but they are memories of ancient man's trust and hope.

The Fremont didn't build their villages very large either—the largest ones had only 10 or 12 houses in use at any one time—but they built them close together. When they found a good stream with tillable land they spread out along it. In some places there were as many as 10 distinct villages in a one-mile stretch. A conglomeration of villages like this may have all belonged to the same clan or, considering the scarcity of water, may have been composed of several clans living in uneasy truce. The Fremont didn't believe in the communal living of the Anasazi. They were more aggressive, more ready to relieve their neighbors of all those worrisome material possessions.

Despite their need to live close to water — which in the high desert is usually found at the bottom of a canyon or arroyo — they placed the villages on high places. If you walk up the Green River north of Green River, Utah, or hike up the Dirty Devil, any hill over 20 feet high and close to farmable land and water is a good bet to have the remnants of a Fremont village. There were several reasons for choosing the high ground to live on. If, for example, you live in a pit-house, it's a good idea to build it where there is good drainage or you might wake up some morning under water. You certainly wouldn't want to build any kind of house, even a sturdy stone one, in the canyon next to the creek, for desert flash floods carry away even modern steel-reinforced concrete bridges.

Land that you live on can't be tilled, and Farmer Fremont needed to farm every available piece of flatland. Some village sites were situated to give a commanding view of the countryside and show evidence of fortification, but these are usually villages that were built in the later period of their occupation. They, same as the Anasazi, were having progressively more trouble with enemies. The fact that these enemies were probably other Fremonts didn't make them any less unfriendly.

Before we had studied the Fremont very much, we made a mistake — not a Classic Blunder, but more a mysterious legend that hasn't completely disappeared yet today. The granaries and storage shelters look like tiny houses just large enough for tiny people to live in. And since we all have a bit of child left in us, we decided there was once a race of people called the Moqui who were about 2 feet tall and lived in "Moqui houses." Farmer Fremont, trotting up to retrieve a stash of corn, would have been scared out of his wits to find a Moqui living in his granary. So, while it is an endearing legend, it simply isn't true.

Since the Fremont didn't have little people to worry about, for the first several hundred years they had their land pretty much to themselves. It was a land rich in natural resources, but the Femont didn't have the technology to exploit it. They made tools and weapons from jasper, chert, flint, chalcedony and obsidian. Ornaments were made from hematite, turquoise and alabaster. They used gilsonite, a tar-like substance, to waterproof their baskets.

The Fremonts did some trading with their neighbors. Mostly they traded for pottery — which is strange since they made quite respectable pots. Mesa Verde and Kayenta potsherds are fairly common at Fremont digs. Pacific ocean olivella shells appear in the ruins of almost every village. They were fond of turquoise, but they must have traded for it since there is no known source of the "sky stone" in their own land. A stone spindle disk found at a ruin between Green River and Watson is a unique anomaly. It is too finely made to be a first-time experiment and its design suggests at least Hohokam manufacture.

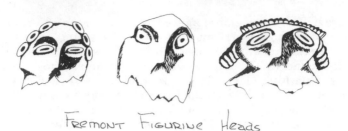

Fremont Figurine Heads

Possibly it even came from the area around Mexico City. When the early Spanish and white settlers came to the Southwest, they found many of these anomalies. It is no wonder that prospectors spent their lives searching for buried Aztec treasure.

Besides homemade and imported spindle whorls, Farmer Fremont made a variety of tools. For cutting tools, he used basically stone, such as flint, and had quite a selection of knives, arrows and saws. He made sickles and scrapers from the horns of mountain sheep and pointed awls from their bones. When his favorite knife broke, he reworked it into a drill. From sandstone, more than plentiful in his land, he made manos, metates and shaft polishers for his arrows. He never needed to cut down the large trees that formed the roof for an Anasazi house or *kiva*, so he didn't develop axes. Some rudimentary specimens have been found but, in general, Farmer Fremont took a tough lump of stone and bludgeoned his way through. One of his less obvious creations was a smoothed ball of stone. The Aztecs played a game with a ball of hard rubber, and the Hohokam adopted ball courts, but Farmer Fremont left no evidence of a ball court. He may have covered the ball with hide, tied the hide to a stick and had a club much like the mace of a medieval knight, but we shall never know for sure. Fire drills, for starting fires from scratch, haven't changed much since the Babylonians used them, and Farmer Fremont saw no reason to innovate in this area: he used a wooden drill and a wooden hearth plate.

In his dress, however, he outpaced his Anasazi neighbors. In the summer, he wore very little, but Utah winters get a bit colder than Pueblo Bonito winters. He didn't rely nearly as much on woven clothing as did the Anasazi, and only a few Fremont bothered to weave sandals.

So what did they wear? Usually, animal hide. Not only is it warmer, but since you have to skin an animal before you cook it anyway, you might as well use that skin for something. They made tough moccasins, robes, breech clouts and other clothing. And they discovered what the Anasazi never hit upon: sewing. Some fragments of leather have been tailored, in what shape we're not sure, but their garments were *worn*, not just draped. Other fragments, unfortunately for Mrs. Fremont, proved that they also discovered mending.

Feather-cloth and fur blankets formed a part of their winter wardrobe, probably a welcome part since temperatures in Fremont land have been recorded as cold as -40 degrees F. Buffalo hide was used for robes and stretched to cover open jars. When it was toughened, it made good shields.

Clothing is a necessity to protect the body; jewelry is a necessity to uplift the spirit. The Fremont lived a more active, aggressive life than the Anasazi so their jewelry is limited mostly to necklaces — a clanking bracelet gets in the way if you are defending your corn crop. The fact that they were proud of their jewelry is proved by their rock art: several rock paintings show figures wearing elaborate jewelry and headdresses.

For materials, they used everything around them that could be carved, woven or strung. Beads and pendants were made of hematite, alabaster and turquoise. Bone was shaped and strung or carved for pendants. Elk teeth were strung for highly-prized necklaces, so highly-prized that some Fremont artisan made "paste" elk teeth by carving them out of bone.

For special occasions, they created special ornaments. Two ceremonial headdresses have been found, both splendid in their barbarity. One was found in a medicine bag made of a deer's face and is a delicate construction of ermine fur and feathers. The other is the top of a deer's head with the eye holes sewn shut and the ears stiffened with feather quills. The man who wore that was a person of great power, probably able to call the deer for good hunting.

Pictographs,
Arches National Park,
Utah.

Their ornaments were impressive but it is in their rock art that the Fremont left their greatest gift to us. The quality and variety of their pictographs are unequalled in North America. The paintings and carvings are so finely executed and — when many of them appear in the same place — so similar, it isn't unreasonable to suspect that they were done by a select group of full-time artists, men whose only job was to record the life of their people, or to glorify the gods with their art.

Fremont pictographs fall into two main types. In type one, the bodies are stiff, ceremoniously posed and shaped like trapezoids. Arms and legs may be just barely indicated, or may not appear at all. Eyes and mouths are blank, hollow. Sometimes lines on the faces suggest ceremonial paint; sometimes the faces are obviously covered by masks. They wear elaborate headdresses, necklaces and pectoral ornaments. In their hands they hold the head of a slain enemy or a fistful of snakes.

Type two are large figures painted in white, red or blue-gray. Their bodies are painted with circles and zig-zag lines or they are covered with decorated robes. They were little jewelry and their eyes are empty.

Some of the figures are painted solid red and have one or two horns on their heads. The modern Hopi have horned *kachinas*, spirits who keep unbelievers away from important ceremonies. Kokopelli is a humpbacked flute player who watches over the Hopi. The Fremont painted his picture several hundred years before the Hopi were a people.

The brilliant Indian civilizations of Mexico raised statues to their gods and carved their likenesses so that all men could see and worship. The only other people on this continent who approached their splendid work were the Fremont. Fremont figurines are elaborate and ornate, molded from clay or carved from wood. Quite often they are found in pairs, male and female, and may represent creator gods. Some seem to have the bodies of men but the heads of birds, and some have been found with grooves cut in the cheeks as if the figures were weeping. Some are the figures of animals or pregnant women. As with pictographs, limbs are practically nonexistent but torso features are well-defined. These small statues have been found wrapped in mats and placed carefully in stone cists. Whatever they represent, they were handled reverently.

The Fremont religion was not as organized as the Anasazi. They built no *kivas* and, in fact, we have found no Fremont structure large enough to contain more than just a few people. Their dance courts may have been the focal point of some ceremony such as the Sun Dance of the latter-day Cheyenne, but we have no proof of this. There is always the chance that Fremont rock art was just friendly gossip but it is more likely that the paintings and carvings are an expression of their religion. Modern Pueblo Indians use snakes in a rain invocation ceremony. It's possible that the Fremont also connected snakes with rain. Paintings of bighorn sheep were almost certainly invocations to the animal spirits for successful hunting. The figurines — particularly the voluptuous female ones—were probably fertility gods and goddesses. To a people in the culture stage of the Fremont, children are not only blessings, they are welcome additions to the labor force.

Fremont figurines were often sealed up in cists inside their houses. Since the Fremont built no temples or *kivas*, it is possible that each household conducted its own ceremonies. The houses where the figures have been found could have been the houses of priests or witch-doctors but this is doubtful. A hunting-farming economy couldn't have supported that many "non-productive" citizens. There is also the possibility that the figurines represented the people themselves, but it is more likely that the figurines were the gods and such an important part of life that the people wanted them close.

When a man went to meet his gods, he didn't take much with him. The Fremont didn't use refuse heaps for burials and we haven't found a great many graves yet, but where we have found them, very few artifacts appear. Farmer Fremont wasn't as supplied with material things as were his Anasazi cousins. This may be because of their beliefs or it may be the result of living in a culture less rich in tangible objects. If you have many pots and baskets and sandals and such, you are more likely to take them with you; if you have few, they are probably shared with the village after you die.

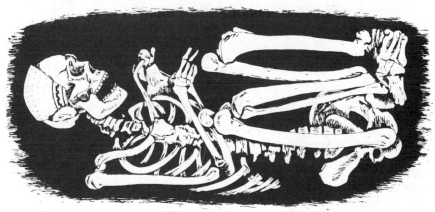

Fremont Burial

Bodies were buried lying on their sides with their knees bent, with only one person to a grave, but one double burial has been found; the bones of an adult and a child were interred together, victims of some ancient tragedy. Graves were often lined with stone and the body was covered with a stone slab before being covered with dirt. Sometimes they buried their dead in rock shelters or caves. In Nine Mile Canyon, northeast of Price, Utah, a cist burial was found next to a burned house. The plains Indians of the 1800's destroyed the dead man's tipi; possibly the Fremont burned his house. Primitive societies often destroy the dead man's home so that his spirit won't hang around.

Farmer Fremont had a tougher life than the Anasazi. He lived in a harsher land with more aggressive neighbors and life — mere survival — was more of a struggle. From birth to death, the majority of his time was used in gathering food. He took time off to worship his gods and create more little Fremonts, but he didn't have the luxury of leisure time as did the people of the large pueblos.

What little free time he did have, he used to play games. Gaming pieces have been found that give us a good idea of what his favorite game was. Flat pieces of bone with different marks on them were Farmer Fremont's dice. Stone disks and pottery sherds were counters. The fall of the dice determined how many spaces the counters could be moved. Sound familiar? The Hopi and Cheyenne play a similar game and, though the dice are cubes and the counters colored plastic, we can find the same type of game in any toy store today.

When he got tired of that game, he may have used those unidentified stone balls to play another. The balls are often found on flatrock that has had pits chipped out: a perfect set-up for a game of marbles, except that a Fremont marble weighed several pounds.

Getting together for an evening of gaming and gambling may have been a major production for Farmer Fremont and friends. His nearest neighbors may have been a couple of canyons away. Many Fremont villages consisted of 4 or 5 houses, just enough to shelter an extended family of uncles and brothers, but in many places one house sits by itself. They simply didn't have the congregating urge of the Anasazi. The settlements were close enough, however, that the fields could be worked by communal labor and the storage towers defended, but they just didn't want to live on top of each other. This settlement pattern is one of the major differences between the Anasazi and the Fremont. To draw a more modern analogy, in the early 1800s most Americans lived on the East Coast. They occupied large cities and were rich in creature comforts. The pioneers who struck off into the Western wilderness lived by themselves, often several families in the same area but far enough apart to have some space around them. Their lives were not as rich in material possessions, but they were a hardy people, efficient in adversity.

If there was one thing Farmer Fremont was used to, it was adversity. But he did pretty well, nonetheless. He established a stable life in the middle of the desert: he grew his crops and painted his pictographs and raised his children. Everything considered, his life was going very well.

THE OLD WAYS CHANGE

And then the drought came. Not only was there less rainfall, but as the mountain glaciers retreated, there was less water in the spring runoff. If the Anasazi lands, where there was more water to begin with, dried up, then Farmer Fremont's lands blew away as dust. And again, as the water went, so did the game. By about 1200 A.D., Farmer Fremont was left with no water for farming and little game to hunt. At this point, he didn't have too many choices open to him.

He could sit where he was, farming less and less, bringing back less meat from the hunt, getting hungrier and dying. But the Fremont were a young, aggressive culture and it is doubtful that they just gave up and died.

He could gather up a few belongings and flee his arid land, find another group of people and join them. If he had done that, some archaeological evidence should remain, and we haven't found any. Also, a village that was already having trouble feeding itself would take a dim view of a bunch of strangers showing up and wanting to share.

So if he didn't give up and he didn't join up, what did he do? We're back to the archaeological guessing game, but the best bet is that Farmer Fremont became Warrior Fremont. Rather than break his back and his hope by farming unfarmable land, Warrior Fremont turned his energy to hunting and became a nomad. He followed the animals and his wanderings took him south. And what was sitting in his path?

The rich pueblos of Mesa Verde and Kayenta and Chaco Canyon. The Shoshonean raiders were basically Warrior Fremont and his allies. So he may have come full circle. He may have left the Anasazi hundreds of years before in small bands looking for another way of life. Now he returned to raid and harass them and, ultimately, drive them from their cliff-houses and pueblos. This life suited the Fremont so well that, in time, they became Utes, a family of Indians so fierce that whites and other Indians alike thought twice before invading their territory. They found horses and rediscovered the lance; they hunted buffalo and chased wagon trains. Until the pressure of white civilization overwhelmed them and placed them on government reservations, they lived a warrior's life. They created no great cities, no written language; their rock art lost its brilliance. But Warrior Fremont lived a life unequalled in its freedom. From a rag-tag scattering of families who farmed the barren lands of Utah, they became people who walked with pride and faced the sun.

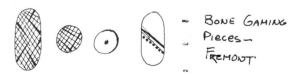

BONE GAMING
Pieces —
FREMONT

Single figure from a panel of Fremont petroglyphs, Capitol Reef National Park, Utah.

CULTURAL SUBDIVISIONS

Anasazi Rock Art
Tsegi Canyon

ANASAZI

At the height of their culture, the Anasazi were the most spectacular of southwestern prehistoric Indians. When they left their pueblos and moved south, they retraced the path their cultural ideas traveled a millenium before.

If the Fertile Crescent was the center of civilization in the ancient eastern world, Mesoamerica was the birthplace of civilization in the Americas. From the areas now known as southern Mexico and Guatemala, ideas spread north and south, influencing people as far away as South America and the eastern coast of North America. Possibly the most important of these ideas was how to grow corn, thereby ensuring a stable food supply and the leisure to create a civilization. Other ideas, from jewelry to religion, also took the same trails.

Considering the distance from Mesoamerica to Anasazi land, it is doubtful that any one person ever made the trip. If the land between had been empty, the Anasazi would probably never have developed as they did. But the land was not empty.

By the standards of life a thousand years ago, the Anasazi were living in the midst of a highly populous country, surrounded by neighbors. To the north were the Fremont whose culture, being farther from the civilized center of Mexico, was in an earlier stage than the Anasazi. To the south, in a basket-like arc cradling the Anasazi, were the Cohonino, Sinagua, Hohokam and Mogollon peoples. (See the regional map on the inside front cover.)

Mayan ruins at Tulum, Yucatan Peninsula, Quintana Roo, Mexico.

Cultural ideas that originated in Mexico traveled slowly north, were filtered through these people, were changed and added to, and finally arrived at Anasazi doors. The Anasazi took these ideas, expanded them to fit their own lifestyles, then gave them back again to the other southwestern tribes. Why the Anasazi rose higher than their neighbors is unknown.

The Cohonino of west central Arizona are the stepchildren of southwestern archaeology. They left few remains and more scientific effort has been directed toward the richer finds in Anasazi land.

Around present-day Flagstaff lived the Sinagua. They were also pueblo-builders, but their architectural style and methods were inferior to Anasazi pueblos. They farmed and kept turkeys but never gathered in cities. They made utilitarian pottery but imported fancy pottery from the Anasazi. By modern standards, their civilization never approached the sophistication of places like Pueblo Bonito and Betatakin.

The Hohokam of the Salt River drainage in southcentral Arizona show the purest evidence of cultural influence from Mesoamerica. They had ball courts, three-legged pots, stone ear-plugs, and copper bells—all items that were prevalent in Mexico. It is possible that some of their religious ceremonies were patterned on the Mexican Indian worship of Quetzalcoatl and the Tlalacs rain god. They farmed and created an extensive system of irrigation canals, some of them 30 miles long. They didn't build Anasazi-type pueblos but their pit houses were so much more comfortable that they may never have felt the need to change.

The Mogollon, who lived on the line between Arizona and New Mexico just south of the midway point, are both the oldest and most stable of southwestern Indians. Their land was farmed as early as 3000 B.C. and the beginning date of a culture recognizable as Mogollon is around 300 B.C. In a way, they are the cultural ancestors of all the ancient southwestern Indians. They were the pottery makers: one style of pottery was continued basically unchanged for 1000 years. The lack of desire to change simply for the sake of change is a hallmark of the Mogollons. They farmed, lived in pit houses, and made pottery in the same way their ancestors did for most of their history. Only in the late stages of Anasazi culture did the Mogollons accept the ideas of stone masonry and black-on-white pottery design.

So the Anasazi had neighbors who were in some ways like them, and in some ways unlike them. The Anasazi themselves were sometimes not like themselves. We have spoken of the Anasazi as a culture, a group of people that shared certain traits. While that is true, it must be remembered that within the culture-group "Anasazi," there were internal differences. There are many reasons for these differences, including the geographic location, local climate, and character of the people, themselves. Because of these differences, the Anasazi are commonly divided into 6 sub-groups: Rio Grande, Little Colorado, Virgin, Kayenta, Chaco and Mesa Verde. (See the map on page 93 for the approximate ranges of these sub-groups.)

The Rio Grande Anasazi lived along the Rio Grande River and its tributaries in north central New Mexico. They may have visited the people of Mesa Verde quite often since it is probable that the Mesa Verde Anasazi moved there after deserting Mesa Verde and Aztec. Two currently occupied pueblos, Acoma and Taos, are in the area inhabited by the prehistoric Rio Grande Anasazi.

If the Cohonino are the stepchildren of southwestern archaeology, then the Little Colorado people are the stepchildren of Anasazi archaeology. They lived in east central Arizona along the Little Colorado River and shared so many cultural traits with the Mogollon, we sometimes aren't exactly certain where the Mogollon left off and the Anasazi began.

The Virgin Anasazi ranged over northern Arizona and southern Utah, west of the Colorado River. For some time, a question existed as to whether they were really Anasazi, since many of their cultural traits are more like the Fremont Indians of Utah. They seemed to have formed a boundary between the sophisticated Kayenta Anasazi and the rougher life of the Fremont.

The Kayenta Anasazi built cliff houses and pueblos in northeast Arizona. Purists may argue a lack of sophistication in their architecture, but their pottery was unexcelled. Pieces of Kayenta pots have been found all over Anasazi land.

Pueblo Bonito was the brightest flowering of Anasazi architecture. The Chaco Anasazi of northwestern New Mexico were the architectural wizards of their culture. The history of European architecture is the history of religion. The same may be true of the Anasazi since the Chaco peoples constructed not only the best pueblos, but also the most *kivas*.

The last subculture group of the Anasazi is the Mesa Verde people. Their center was Four Corners and they lived in all four states: Utah, Colorado, New Mexico and Arizona. They were potters, though not as good as the Kayenta; they were builders, though not as good as the Chaco. But they left us Cliff Palace, now a highlight at Mesa Verde National Park.

Unrestored Una Vida ruins, Chaco Canyon National Monument, New Mexico.

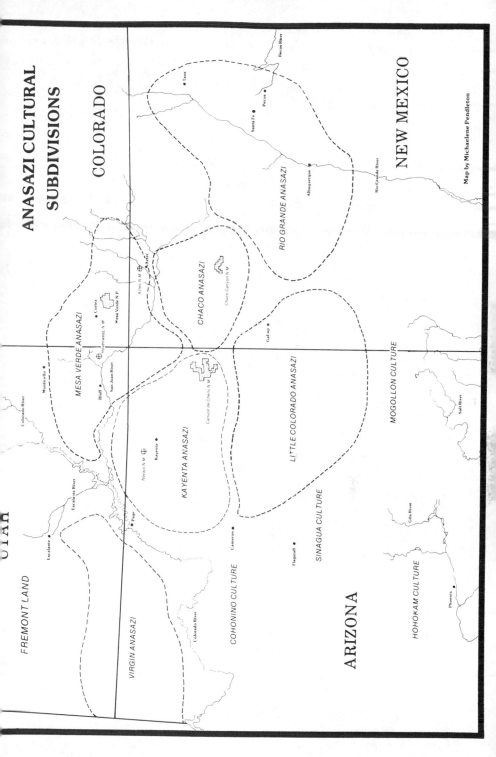

ANASAZI CULTURAL SUBDIVISIONS

COLORADO

NEW MEXICO

UTAH

ARIZONA

FREMONT LAND

VIRGIN ANASAZI

COHONINO CULTURE

KAYENTA ANASAZI

MESA VERDE ANASAZI

CHACO ANASAZI

RIO GRANDE ANASAZI

LITTLE COLORADO ANASAZI

SINAGUA CULTURE

MOGOLLON CULTURE

HOHOKAM CULTURE

Colorado River
Escalante River
Escalante
Page
Colorado River
Cameron
Flagstaff
Montivello
Bluff
San Juan River
Navajo N M
Kayenta
Canyon de Chelly N M
Gallup
Cortez
Mesa Verde N P
Hovenweep N M
Aztec N M
Chaco Canyon N M
Albuquerque
Rio Grande River
Santa Fe
Pecos
Taos
Pecos River
Salt River
Gila River
Phoenix

Map by Michaelene Pendleton

93

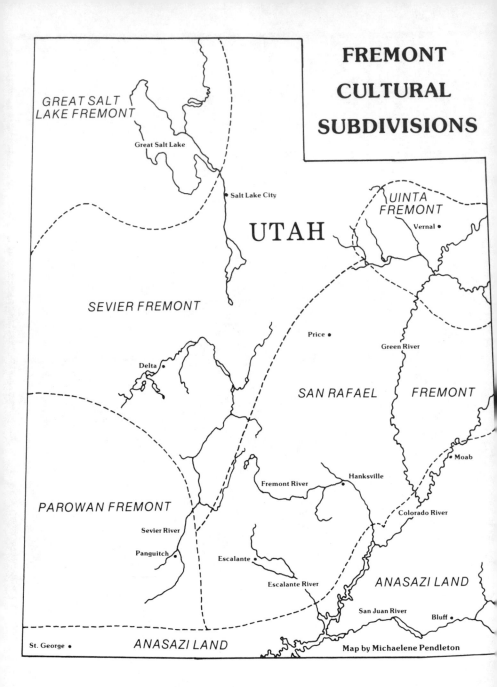

FREMONT CULTURAL SUBDIVISIONS

GREAT SALT LAKE FREMONT

Great Salt Lake

Salt Lake City

UTAH

UINTA FREMONT

Vernal ●

SEVIER FREMONT

Price ●

Green River

Delta ●

SAN RAFAEL

FREMONT

● Moab

PAROWAN FREMONT

Fremont River

Hanksville

Colorado River

Sevier River

Panguitch ●

Escalante ●

Escalante River

ANASAZI LAND

San Juan River

Bluff ●

St. George ●

ANASAZI LAND

Map by Michaelene Pendleton

94

FREMONT

Just as the Anasazi had subcultures within the main culture-group "Anasazi," so the Fremont are divided into 5 different groups. (See the map on page 94 for the approximate ranges of these groups.)

The Parowan Fremont lived in the Parowan Valley of south-western Utah, their lands bordering the areas of the Virgin and Kayenta Anasazi. They occupied this area from approximately 900 to 1300 A.D. Two things that differentiate them from their brothers is that they made wide-mouth pottery jars and painted their figurines red.

The Sevier Fremont lived in west central Utah from about 760 to 1260 A.D. About the only way to tell the Seviers from the rest of the Fremonts is by their flint work: they made large, leaf-shaped blades.

The shortest-lived Fremont were the Uintas. They occupied the Uinta Basin in northeastern Utah for only 300 years, from 650 to 950 A.D. The way to tell Uintas from other Fremonts is by their pottery: it's all gray. They never made figurines and they used a different kind of metate.

The San Rafael Fremont ranged from central Utah southwest to the Colorado River and shared a boundary with the Mesa Verde Anasazi from around 700 to 1200 A.D. They traded for Mesa Verde and Kayenta pottery while making artistic pottery of their own. In places such as the Escalante River drainage in southcentral Utah, they traded occupancy with the Virgin and Kayenta Anasazi.

The Great Salt Lake Fremont were least like their brothers. They lived on the lake's saline shore from 400 to 1350 A.D., hunting more and farming less. Their projectile points are most reminiscent of the ancestral Desert Archaic style and they show fewer indicators of culture exchange with the Anasazi.

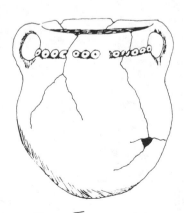

UINTA FREMONT JAR

CULTURAL NEIGHBORS

The Anasazi and Fremont, the two prehistoric cultures that occupied canyon country, may be likened to modern American society: they were peoples who had neighbors with whom they shared some traits, yet they were as different from each other as a New Englander and a Southwesterner. As we view civilization, they were among the most civilized prehistoric Indians of the North American continent. Our society would be poorer were it not for the ruins, art, and relics they left to enrich us.

Pictographs in the Horseshoe Canyon annex of Canyonlands National Park, Utah.

A CULTURAL CALENDAR

In our modern world, if we want to know when an event took place, we can look up the date in a yearly almanac or an old newspaper file. An archaeologist studying prehistoric Indians is not so fortunate. Scientific research on the Anasazi began in earnest in the 1880s, but it wasn't until 1927 that an archaeological calendar was agreed upon by most of the scientific community.

At Pecos, New Mexico, a conference was held in the late summer of 1927. Many of the experts on Southwestern archaeology attended and, among other things, agreed on a standardized cultural calendar. Although it has been slightly modified since, as new discoveries have been made, the Pecos Classification is the calendar used today to chart the Anasazi culture.

In its pure form, the Pecos Classification is not a *time* calendar, but an agreement on which cultural traits combine to signify a certain period. For example, when Anasazi houses moved above ground, this was significant enough to call that period in the culture "Pueblo I," thus indicating an advance from "Basketmaker III." Since some villages operated at one cultural stage while villages a few miles away operated at another, it is not scientifically accurate to speak of the entire culture as being at a particular stage. An archaeological research paper on a particular site could refer with some authority to a period within the Pecos Classification, but a reputable scientist would not generalize from his dig to claim that all Anasazi culture was at the same stage.

Some years after the 1927 conference, generalized dates were given to the Pecos Classification system, although within the scientific community there are disagreements of 100 years or more on transition dates. This has two basic reasons: 1. the aforementioned problem of changes in different places at different times, and 2. the difficulty sometimes of knowing exactly when one period ended and another began.

The Pecos Classification covers eight periods of prehistoric Indian development. In this book some of these periods have been combined at the discretion of the author. Since this current treatment of the subject is not as detailed as a scientific assessment of one particular site, but is an attempt to give an overall picture of Anasazi life, a different terminology from the Pecos Classification has been used. The following is a list of the main areas covered in this book and how they relate to the Pecos Classification:

In the Beginning, pre - 1 AD:
  Pecos Classification: Basketmaker I.
  This period covers the beginning of man's residence in the Southwest and includes the Archaic Desert Culture.

Basketmakers, 1 to 500 AD:
   Pecos Classification: Basketmaker II.
   Here begins the culture known as the Anasazi. The people lived usually in small groups, often in caves; grew corn and squash; hunted with spears, and made fine baskets.
Modified Basketmakers, 500 to 700 AD:
   Pecos Classification: Basketmaker III.
   Established villages emerged; pithouses were built; pottery was discovered; beans became part of the food supply; and bows and arrows were used.
Early Pueblos, 700 to 1100 AD:
   Pecos Classification: Pueblo I and Pueblo II.
   The Anasazi adopted a hard cradleboard; houses moved above ground and were joined into units; *kivas* went below ground; basketry declined; cotton was used for cloth.
The Great Years, 1100 to 1200 AD:
   Pecos Classification: Pueblo III.
   This period ends in the middle of Pueblo III, about 1200 AD. The Anasazi congregated into large communities and built multi-storied pueblos; and craft specialization began.
Cultural Decline, 1200 to 1598 AD:
   Pecos Classification: Pueblo III and Pueblo IV.
   This period begins in the middle of Pueblo III.
   Pressure from enemies and the changing climate marked the end of the great pueblos. The people moved and blended with other cultures. The arrival of Spanish explorers in the mid-1500s heralded historic times. Pueblo V is dated from 1598 AD to the present but is not covered in this book.
   A Fremont calendar roughly parallels that of the Anasazi. Though their cultural indicators are quite different, the earliest date that can definitely be applied to the prehistoric Indians we call the Fremont is around 400 A.D. And like the Anasazis, they, as a concentrated culture, disappeared around 1300 A.D., probably for the same reasons.
   While much care has been taken to provide a reasonably accurate calendar, the reader is advised that, at any time, an archaeological discovery may render parts of it inaccurate. (For a graphic presentation of the cultural calendar just described, see the inside back cover of this book.)

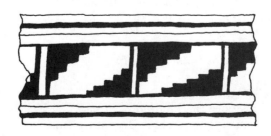

RUINS
by
F. A. Barnes

Introduction

Listing of Ruin Sites
Photographs

Canyon-rim Anasazi tower, Hovenweep National Monument, Utah.

INTRODUCTION

Isolated canyon-rim ruins, Hovenweep National Monument, Utah.

REMNANTS

The surviving remnants of the prehistoric Anasazi and Fremont cultures fall into three general categories: ruins, artifacts and rock art. Of these, the most apparent to canyon country visitors, be they early explorers or present-day tourists, are the ruins—the remains of structures.

RUINS DEFINED

The term "ruin" can be defined narrowly, meaning major cliff dwellings only, or it can be defined broadly, as in this book, to mean any remaining trace of any type of prehistoric structure, of whatever material, located anywhere, and used for whatever purpose by its builders. Such structures may have been built from rock, sticks, brush, logs, mud and in existing cliffs, caves or alcoves, and in any combination. They may have been used as dwellings, ceremonial chambers, graves, trash dumps, food bins, lookout towers, defense walls, turkey pens, irrigation systems, temporary shelters, or for pure decoration. They may have been located in caves or shallow alcoves, just below such natural shelters, in open valleys, on knolls, on the tops of mesas or the rims of cliffs, or perched upon gigantic boulders or slabs or rock.

Such ruins have long been the most apparent to canyon country visitors, from early explorers to modern tourists, especially those of the larger dwelling sites or pueblos. "Pueblo" is the Spanish word for "town." Ruins, as broadly defined, are found throughout the Anasazi and Fremont cultural areas, although almost all of the larger, more sophisticated dwelling ruins are Anasazi. Fremont dwellings were generally far simpler in construction and have not survived the ravages of time very well.

In addition to the more conspicuous pueblos and cliff dwellings, there are many hundreds of dwelling ruins within the general Four Corners region that housed from one to a few families. Most of these are located in remote areas that are not easy to penetrate. Some are cliff dwellings, some stand in open country. Some that were located in the open have been partially or completely covered by sediments, drifting sand or dust, or accumulating plant humus. Many that were built near perennial or seasonal stream courses have been damaged or totally destroyed by stream bank erosion. Most such erosion was caused by recent agricultural efforts that have damaged watersheds and promoted rapid, destructive runoff.

Another type of ruin commonly found throughout canyon country is the stone-and-mud food storage chamber. These are generally on elevated stone ledges that are protected from rain by overhanging rock. They usually have small openings that were closed by flat slabs of rock or by more mud and smaller stones. Such small structures with their tiny "doors" gave rise to the canyon country legend of the "Moki," or the tiny people who once lived in these "dwellings."

In fact, such sealable cists were used for the storage of cultivated or gathered foods that could stand prolonged storage, such as grains, wild seeds and tubers. The cists protected such provisions from rain, insects and small animals. When located in hidden places remote from dwelling sites, they even saved scarce food from human thieves.

Detail of outside wall, Pueblo Bonito ruins, Chaco Canyon National Monument, New Mexico.

101

PROTECTION

Although virtually all of the major dwelling ruins were first stripped of artifacts by private and commercial collectors, the dwellings themselves — those that survived the illegal excavating — were of no value to the collectors so they were left behind. Most of these have since been studied by archaeologists, restored to some degree, stabilized against further collapse, and made accessible to the public within national and state park areas.

Such protected park areas may also have dwelling ruins in their more remote reaches that are still in their natural condition, but accessible only by hiking or off-road vehicle. Similar ruins also occur in special federal and state areas such as historic monuments, recreation areas and primitive areas.

In contrast to the major ruins that are now protected, there are thousands of dwellings and other ruins within the canyon country hinterlands that receive little or no practical protection, even though they may be on public land administered by federal or state agencies. Fortunately, most such ruins are difficult to find and enter. This, plus the fact that they have long since been stripped of obvious artifacts by generations of hobby and commercial collectors, preserves most of these ruins from further human destruction. Even this protection, however, is diminishing, as the mineral industry bulldozes more and more roads into remote canyon country, and these roads are used by the more destructive collectors and vandals to reach the many unprotected archaeological sites.

Some of the more obvious backcountry ruins have at least been surveyed and their positions recorded by teams of archaeological field workers, but most of these have not yet been studied in any depth, if at all. Countless thousands of other less conspicuous ruins, many of them even buried or partially buried, have neither been recorded nor studied. The Anasazi-Fremont region is simply too large and wild, and neither land administration agencies nor the institutions charged with the study of antiquities have been adequately funded for such an endeavor. As a result, irretrievable losses continue, despite a number of laws that give theoretical protection to antiquities.

EARLY DISCOVERIES

Early explorers who entered the general Four Corners region were the first to report the prehistoric ruins there. As the famous Dominguez-Escalante Expedition out of Santa Fe reached the vicinity of the present town of Dolores, in southwestern Colorado, Escalante reported on August 13, 1776, that:

"Upon an elevation on the river's south side, there was in ancient times a small settlement of the same type as those of the Indians of New Mexico, as the ruins which we purposely inspected show."

The river noted is the present Dolores River, where a huge reservoir is now being built. One of the ruins Escalante saw will be excavated and preserved, but many others will be lost, sacrificed to an irrigation project.

The Macomb Expedition of 1859 also started from Santa Fe and at first closely followed the route of the Dominguez-Escalante Expedition. In southwestern Colorado, the Macomb Expedition reported finding extensive prehistoric ruins near its Camp 21, which was just above the confluence of the Dolores and Mancos rivers. The expedition's geologist, a Professor J. S. Newberry, climbed a nearby hill and reported "an extensive series of very ancient ruins," one a pueblo "nearly 100 feet square" which he then described in detail. His report also noted other ruins in the vicinity.

As the Macomb Expedition neared its principal goal, the deeply imbedded, canyon-guarded confluence of the Green and Colorado rivers, a small party from the group headed down a narrow, tortuous gorge, hoping it would allow access to the deep inner Colorado River gorge and hence to the confluence. They named this gorge "Labyrinth Canyon." Newberry, one of this detachment, noted that:

"Some two miles below the head of Labyrinth Canyon we came upon the ruins of a large number of houses of stone, evidently built by the Pueblo Indians, as they are similar to those on the Dolores, and the pottery scattered about is identical with that before found in so many places. It is very old but of excellent quality, made of red clay coated with white, and handsomely figured. Here the houses are built in the sides of the cliffs. A mile or two below we saw others crowning the inaccessible summits — inaccessible except by ladders — of picturesque detached buttes of red sandstone, which rise to the height of one hundred and fifty feet above the bottom of the canyon. Similar buildings were found lower down, and broken pottery was picked up upon the summits of the cliffs overhanging Grand River (now the Colorado River), evidence that these dreadful canyons were once the homes of families belonging to that great people

Sketch of ruins in "Labyrinth Canyon," as reported by members of the historic Macomb Expedition.

formerly spread all over this region now so utterly sterile, solitary, and desolate."

Professor Newberry made rough sketches of some of these ruins, and one sketch was later rendered in detail by a professional artist. Today, Newberry's "Labyrinth Canyon," renamed Indian Creek Canyon, lies partly within the Needles District of Canyonlands National Park, partly in surrounding federal land administered by the Bureau of Land Management. Many of the ruins first sighted by Macomb Expedition members can still be viewed by hikers, although all the lovely pottery described by Newberry has long since vanished into private collections.

Major John Wesley Powell's account of his 1869 exploration down the Green and Colorado rivers records hundreds of prehistoric ruins throughout the general canyon country region. Both Anasazi and Fremont ruins are described — although these cultural names were not in use then — plus the many dwellings of the Indian tribes that occupied parts of the region at that time.

In the overview chapters of his book, when describing the area that is now the northeastern corner of Arizona, Powell notes that:

"Perhaps the most interesting ruins of America are found in this region. The ancient pueblos found here are of superior structure, but they were built by a people whom the Navajos displaced when they migrated from the far North. Wherever there is water, nearby an ancient ruin may be found, and these ruins are gathered about centers, the centers being larger pueblos and the scattered ruins representing single houses. The ancient people lived in villages, or pueblos, but during the growing season they scattered about by the springs and streams to cultivate the soil by irrigation, and wherever there was a little farm or garden patch, there was built a summer house of stone. When times of war came, especially when they were invaded by the Navajos, these ancient people left their homes in the pueblos and by the streams and constructed temporary homes in the cliffs and canyon walls. Such cliff ruins are abundant throughout the region. Ultimately the ancient pueblo peoples succumbed to the prowess of the Navajos and were driven out."

These ruins were Anasazi, but the same Powell account also mentioned Fremont ruins in what is now northeastern Utah.

"The Uinta Valley is the ancient and present home of the Uinta Indians.... In this valley there are also found many ruins of ancient pueblo-building peoples of what stock is not known."

The daily log of the 1869 Powell expedition noted the discovery of some ruins beside the Colorado River in a stretch that Powell named Glen Canyon.

"July 29. We enter a canyon today with low, red walls. A short distance below its head we discover the ruins of an old building on the left wall. There is a narrow plain between the river and the wall just here, and on the brink of a rock 200 feet high stands this old house. Its walls are of stone, laid in mortar with much regularity. It was probably built three stories high; the lower story is yet almost intact; the second is much broken down, and scarcely anything is left of the third. Great quantities of flint chips are found on the rocks near by, and many arrowheads, some perfect, others broken; and fragments of pottery are strewn about in great profusion. On the face of the cliff, under the building and along down the river for 200 or 300 yards, there are many interesting etchings. Two hours are given to the examination of these interesting ruins; then we run down fifteen miles farther, and discover another group."

Powell then describes this second group of ruins in detail, including a kiva. Frederick S. Dellenbaugh, in his account of the second Powell expedition in 1871 also notes numerous ruins along the Colorado River in Glen Canyon.

All of these ruins are now deep beneath the dark waters of Lake Powell, lost forever to the eyes of man. Not even draining this man-made lake, as some have advocated, would recover these inundated remnants of the prehistoric Anasazis. Thick, mucky sediment has long since deeply buried what the water has not completely destroyed.

Powell also reported one aspect of the impact our modern culture was having on prehistoric ruins:

> "The Kanab River heading in the Pink Cliffs runs directly southward and joins the Colorado in the heart of the Grand Canyon. Its way is through a series of canyons. From one of these it emerges at the foot of the Vermilion Cliffs, and here stood an extensive ruin not many years ago. Some portions of the pueblo were three stories high. The structure was one of the best found in this land of ruins. The Mormon people settling here have used the stones of the old pueblo in building their homes, and now no vestiges of the ancient structure remain."

In 1874, the "Hayden Survey," officially called the "U.S. Geological and Geographic Survey of the Territories," penetrated the Four Corners region. There, William H. Jackson took the first photographs of a Mesa Verde cliff dwelling, and named it "Two Story House." Subsequent surveying and exploring groups sponsored by the federal government or private industry also reported many prehistoric ruins in the region, as did early Mormon scouts and pioneer settlers.

In December of 1879, scouts for the Mormon pioneer group that became known for its perilous descent into the Colorado River gorge through the "Hole-in-the-Rock," came upon an unexpected lake in the midst of the sand-and-slickrock wilderness that dominates the high terrain between the Colorado and San Juan rivers near their confluence. This highly unusual lake, which has since disappeared, showed signs of sporadic use by historic Indian tribes, but also had a number of prehistoric Anasazi ruins along its shores and nearby. Later research indicated heavy, continuous occupancy of this site from about 1000 to 1275 A.D.

Local Paiute Indians called this unique lake "Pagahrit," or "standing water." The strange story of its origin and demise is summarized in the book "Canyon Country Geology."

SCIENTIFIC RESEARCH

Early scientific research centering on Anasazi and Fremont prehistoric ruins began in the 1880s, but for the next twenty-five or thirty years was widely scattered, sporadic, uncoordinated and largely very unscientific. Most of it was simply random, spotty digging for the more conspicuous artifacts, with little or no system. In the Anasazi region, study was largely confined to the more spectacular cliff dwellings and pueblos. In the Fremont territory, most of the less sophisticated ruins had been reduced by the elements to uninspiring mounds of dirt and rocky rubble, and scientific work on these around the turn of the century was sparse and scattered.

Beginning in the 1920s, several major archaeological surveys and excavations in both cultural areas put scientific research on its first sound basis. During the following decades, such archaeologists as Kidder, Judd, Harrington, Hayden, Steward and Morse did extensive field work on the two canyon country prehistoric cultures, and developed cultural images that have survived virtually intact to the present.

Some of the archaeological papers and books listed under SOURCES contain detailed histories of this early research, as well as extensive bibliographies of publications summarizing the research findings.

Oddly, in recent years, the scientific world seems to have been more preoccupied with matters other than the archaeology of the general Four Corners region. Most of the recent work with ruins there has been salvage work just ahead of some big industrial development, with both time and funds quite limited.

There is some ongoing work with the ruins at various protected sites, such as in federal and state parks, but long-range, systematic, culture-wide programs are non-existent. Most of the unprotected ruins in remote areas, especially those that can be reached and excavated only with considerable effort and expense, remain untouched by archaeologists, with little prospect for their study in the forseeable future.

ARCHITECTURE AND AGE

Anasazi and Fremont structures vary drastically in architectural style, materials, use and durability. Architectural styles vary from simple stick-and-mud huts, to airtight masonry food-storage cists, to poorly designed rock-walled huts, to magnificent cliff dwellings and even a few log structures reminiscent of pioneer log cabins. Some structures were even built partly or completely underground, such as kivas, or burial crypts and food-storage cists lined with stone slabs and sealed with mud.

Materials were limited to whatever was locally available. In most of the general Four Corners region this was sandstone, logs, small sticks, brush and mud. In some locations, local minerals added to the mud improved its quality as mortar, and the types of trees available in quantity affected structural design.

The tools to work these materials were, of course, quite crude. This also tended to place limits on how effectively even these simple materials could be used. The logs could be cut and shaped to some extent with sharp stone axes, but could not be sawed into slabs or planks, nor drilled for joining with pegs. Rock could easily be broken into smaller pieces, but shaping it with tools of harder stone involved more labor and time than canyon country Indians had to expend.

As noted earlier, the uses of structures varied widely, from dwellings to graves, from trash dumps to food-storage cists, animal pens and seasonal field shelters. Because of these diverse uses, the structures were built in locations that afforded varying amounts of protection. Thus, several factors worked together to determine the long-range durability of prehistoric canyon country human structures. These factors — style, materials and use — together with time, the natural elements and our own culture's impact upon them, have all affected the survival of the thousands of structures left behind by the Anasazi and Fremont cultures as identifiable "ruins" that can be now studied and appreciated by archaeologists and canyon country visitors.

Details concerning the architectural styles used by these early Formative stage Amerinds could easily fill an entire book, but here it is enough to note the major variables and how these affected a structure's survival to the present. In general, if a dwelling was well built, made of inorganic materials such as rock and mud, and located where it was sheltered from the elements, it tended to survive almost unchanged over the centuries. Where logs were used as critical structural elements, survival of the structure was poor in the open, but better in locations sheltered from the moisture that promoted wood decay. Even in caves and sheltered alcoves, however, logs tended to rot and fall, or to be weakened by insects, and thus allowed the collapse of rock walls.

Smaller limbs and brush, when used in structures, tended to fail much faster than logs, especially in locations exposed to weather and moisture. Thus, most of the older structures that relied heavily on these materials were destroyed by the elements long before historic times. With more recent structures — where such smaller plant materials was used with mud to make floors and ceilings in multi-storied dwellings — if the dwelling was sheltered in a dry cave, some of it survived to the present. But with dwellings built in the open, rot and collapse were almost certain.

The elements, however, often destroyed even the most sturdy structures, or buried them from view. Given time, canyon country winds can and do completely obliterate major features, including stone

Interior detail, Pueblo Bonito ruin, Chaco Canyon National Monument, New Mexico. Note the charred ends of the timbers that supported the floor of the second story.

pueblos, with drifts of dust and sand. Flash floods can destroy structures under countless tons of rubble, and rock collapses can plunge canyon-rim dwellings into deep gorges.

In the open, and even in caves that have seeping water, the roots of growing plants can slowly but surely topple well-built structures, and persistent rodents, insects and rootlets can penetrate and damage the best made burial crypt or food-storage cist, given time.

Thus, between the natural elements and the depradations of modern man, it is something of a minor miracle that so many Anasazi and Fremont structures have survived to become "ruins."

Until the late 1920s, when an archaeologist found or exhumed such a ruin, it was difficult, if not impossible, to determine its age with any accuracy. The age-dating methods available were little better than educated guesses. All this changed for the better, however, with the development of tree-ring dating, or *dendrochronology*. With this method, if a few wood specimens from a structure are available—such as the log beams in a cliff dwelling—archaeologists can date the structure with amazing precision, sometimes to within a month or so within a particular year. By careful use of this precision age-dating method, archaeologists made tremendous progress in piecing together a much clearer picture of canyon country prehistoric cultures. The basic tree-ring "calendar" used in dendrochronology for southwest historic times was developed during the early 1900s, then finally integrated with the southwestern prehistoric tree-ring "calendar" in 1929. This gave canyon country archaeology an enormous boost, and has since permitted the accurate dating of most major ruins.

Details concerning the theory and practice of tree-ring dating can be found in numerous books and scientific papers, including several of those listed under SOURCES.

LISTING OF RUIN SITES

The ruin sites listed in the following section of this book are all within protected areas that are under federal or state administration. Most are Anasazi ruins, but some are of related cultures that bordered the Anasazi region.

Most are within areas administered by the National Park Service, while a few are within state parks or historic sites, or on land administered by the Bureau of Land Management. All are patrolled by rangers.

Most of the ruins that receive moderate to heavy public visitation are stabilized against further collapse and the normal wear and tear of public viewing. Ruins in some of the more remote parts of the noted areas are not stabilized and should not be entered except in company of an official guide. Guides are also required in some of the major stabilized ruins. Remote ruins that have been stabilized for unguided public entry are generally designated by local interpretive literature or by signs. Scientific studies of some ruins may be in progress. Some may even be temporarily closed to the public during study, restoration or stabilization.

It should be noted that while other protected areas within the Four Corners region — such as Arches, Bryce, Zion and Capitol Reef National Parks; Natural Bridges, Dinosaur and Colorado National Monuments; Dark Canyon Primitive Area, Flaming Gorge National Recreation Area, and several National Forest areas — all contain many archaeological sites, these sites are generally in remote locations, have few ruins of any size and are of interest only to archaeologists. Although these places do not appear in the list of ruins, some of them may have archaeological displays in their museums and thus are listed in the chapter on prehistoric artifacts.

Most of the Indian reservations within the general Four Corners region have prehistoric ruins on them that are accessible only to off-road vehicles accompanied by authorized Indian guides.

To find the ruins within the listed sites and areas, visitors should refer to local literature, maps and guides. Access to the ruins may be easy, by highway vehicle and short walks, or may require off-road vehicles or hiking. Some can be reached only by special tour buses or trucks. Other guide books in the Canyon Country series describe how to reach some of the backcountry ruins in southeastern Utah.

RUINS PHOTOGRAPHS

Some of the photographs of ruins, in the pictorial section that follows the listing of sites, depict major ruins at those sites. Others show representative backcountry ruins that may or may not be within the protected areas listed. Where the ruins shown are not within such protected areas, only their general locations are given. All ruins photographs are by the author of this chapter.

Cave dwellings, Gila Cliff Dwellings National Monument, Utah.

Interior detail, Gila Cliff Dwellings National Monument, New Mexico.

LISTING OF RUIN SITES

STATE	SITE NAME	NEAREST CITIES OR TOWNS	APPROACH HIGHWAYS	ACCESS TO RUINS
ARIZONA	Grand Canyon National Park	Flagstaff and Williams	U.S. 180 & Arizona 64	Highway vehicle and easy walking.
	Petrified Forest National Park	Holbrook or Gallup, N.M.	Interstate 40	Highway vehicle and easy walking.
	Canyon de Chelly National Monument	Chinle	Arizona 63 & Indian Routes 7 & 64	Some sites can be viewed from highway overlooks. Some sites can be reached only by ORV and easy walking. One site can also be reached by highway plus hiking.
	Casa Grande Ruins National Monument	Coolidge	Arizona 87	Highway vehicle and easy walking.
	Montezuma Castle National Monument	Flagstaff or Camp Verde	Interstate 17	Highway vehicle and easy walking.
	Navajo National Monument	Kayenta or Tuba City	U.S. 160 & Arizona 564	Highway vehicle and easy walking.
	Tonto National Monument	Globe	U.S. 60 or Arizona 88	Highway vehicle and hiking.
	Tuzigoot National Monument	Jerome or Cottonwood	U.S. 89A	Highway vehicle and easy walking.

ARIZONA (continued)	Walnut Canyon National Monument	Flagstaff	Interstate 17 or 40 & county road	Highway vehicle and easy walking or hiking.
	Wupatki National Monument	Flagstaff	U.S. 89	Highway vehicle and easy walking or hiking.
	Kinishba Ruins, Fort Apache Indian Reservation	Whiteriver or Carrizo	Arizona 73	Highway vehicle and easy walking. There are other ruins in the reservation backcountry.
	Homolovi Ruins State Park	Winslow	Arizona 87	Highway vehicle and easy walking.
	Casa Malpais Pueblo	Springerville	Arizona 60	Highway vehicle with guide.
COLORADO	Mesa Verde National Park	Cortez or Durango	U.S. 160	Some sites can be reached by highway vehicle and easy walking. Some sites can be viewed from highway overlooks. Some sites can be reached only by park bus.
	Lowry Ruins (BLM)	Cortez or Dove Creek	U.S. 666 & dirt road from Pleasant View	Highway vehicle and easy walking.
	Anasazi Heritage Center	Dolores	Colorado 184	Highway vehicle and easy walking.
	Ute Mountain Tribal Park	Cortez and Tewaoc	U.S. 666	Accessible to visitors with guide hiking or backpacking.

NEW MEXICO			
Aztec Ruins National Monument	Farmington & Aztec	U.S. 550 & local road	Highway vehicle and easy walking.
Bandelier National Monument	Santa Fe or Española	U.S. 84/285 & New Mexico 4	Highway vehicle and easy walking, hiking or backpacking to various sites.
Chaco Culture National Historical Park	Bloomfield or Gallup	Interstate 40 & New Mexico 57	Highway vehicle via long dirt road plus easy walking or hiking.
El Morro National Monument	Gallup or Grants	New Mexico 52 & 53	Highway vehicle and hiking.
Gila Cliff Dwellings National Monument	Silver City	U.S. 180 & New Mexico 15	Highway vehicle and hiking.
Gran Quivira National Monument	Carizozo or Mountainair	U.S. 54 & New Mexico 14	Highway vehicle and easy walking.
Pecos National Monument	Santa Fe or Las Vegas	Interstate 25 & New Mexico 63	Highway vehicle and easy walking.
Abo State Monument	Mountainair or Bernardo	U.S. 60	Highway vehicle and easy walking.
Coronado State Monument	Albuquerque & Bernalillo	U.S. 85 & New Mexico 44	Highway vehicle and easy walking.
Quarai State Monument	Mountainair	U.S. 60	Highway vehicle and easy walking.
Puye Cliff Dwellings	Española	New Mexico 5	Highway vehicle and easy walking.
Salmon Ruins	Farmington	U.S. 64	Short trail from visitor center.

114

UTAH	Canyonlands National Park	Moab or Monticello	U.S. 191, Utah 313 & county road, or Utah 211	One site on Island in the Sky can be reached by highway vehicle and easy walking. Sites in Needles district can be reached only by ORV or hiking.
	Hovenweep National Monument	Blanding or Bluff	U.S. 191, Utah 262 & county road	Some sites can be reached by highway vehicle and easy walking. Other sites require off-road vehicle and/or hiking.
	Glen Canyon National Recreation Area	Blanding or Hanksville	Utah 95, Utah 276, Utah 263 or U.S. 89	All sites are accessible only by boat, plus hiking and/or climbing at some sites.
	Anasazi Indian Village State Historical Monument	Boulder	Utah 12	Highway vehicle and easy walking.
	Edge of the Cedars and West Water Ruins State Historical Monument	Blanding	U.S. 191 & county road	Highway vehicle and easy walking.
	Beef Basin Archaeological Area (BLM)	Moab or Monticello	U.S. 191, Utah 211, & ORV road	All sites are accessible only by off-road vehicle, plus easy walking or hiking.
	Grand Gulch Primitive Area (BLM)	Blanding or Hanksville	Utah 95 & Utah 261	All sites are accessible only by highway vehicle plus backpacking or horseback.

UTAH (continued)			
Montezuma Canyon (BLM)	Bluff or Monticello	U.S. 191, Utah 262 & county road	Upper canyon is gravel road usually passable to highway vehicles. Lower canyon passable only to off-road vehicles. Sites accessible from road either by walking or hiking.
Mule Canyon Ruin (BLM)	Blanding or Hanksville	U.S. 191 & Utah 95	Small ruins at marked highway pullout between junctions of U.S. 191/U95 and U95/U261.
San Juan River, between Bluff and Lake Powell (BLM & Navajo Indian Reservation)	Bluff & Mexican Hat	U.S. 191 & county roads	Various ruins are accessible from the river, when run under BLM permit.

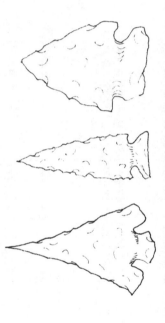

Ruin detail, Gila Cliff Dwellings National Monument, New Mexico

One of several large kivas in Pueblo Bonito ruins, Chaco Canyon National Monument, New Mexico.

Alcove dwelling site, upper Salt Creek Canyon, Canyonlands National Park, Utah. Note pictograph faces above the ruin.

(Left) Ruins of Anasazi canyon-rim dwelling, Hovenweep National Monument, Utah.
(Right) Kiva wall detail, Aztec Ruins National Monument, New Mexico.

(Left) Antelope House ruins, Canyon de Chelly National Monument, Arizona.
(Right) Gila Cliff Dwellings National Monument, New Mexico.

Two-story Anasazi dwelling, Hovenweep National Monument, Utah.

Two-story Anasazi granary under a natural arch, Davis Canyon, Canyonlands National Park, Utah.

West end of Pueblo Bonito ruins, Chaco Canyon National
Monument, New Mexico.

East end of Pueblo Bonito ruins, Chaco Canyon National Monument, New Mexico.
Note that a huge rockfall has damaged the ruin.

Lower White House ruins, Canyon de Chelly National Monument, Arizona.

(Left) Doorway detail, Great Kiva at Casa Rinconada ruin, Chaco Canyon National Monument, New Mexico. Note tunnel entrance below door. (Right) Mesa-top Anasazi ruins, El Morro National Monument, New Mexico.

Canyon-rim view of Casa Rinconada ruin and Great Kiva, Chaco Canyon National Monument, New Mexico.

(Left) Anasazi tower, Ruin Park, Beef Basin Archaeological Area, Utah. (Right) Cave ruins, Gila Cliff Dwellings National Monument, New Mexico.

Mesa-top Anasazi ruins at Edge of the Cedars State Historical Monument, Utah, Abajo Mountains in the background.

Pueblo del Arroyo ruins, Chaco Canyon National Monument, New Mexico.

Cliff-dwelling, Gila Cliff Dwellings National Monument, New Mexico.

Lower ruins, White House ruins, Canyon de Chelly National Monument, Arizona.

Room detail, Pueblo Bonito ruin, Chaco Canyon National Monument, New Mexico.

Anasazi cave-dwelling, Fish Creek Canyon, Utah.

Anasazi dwelling, Hovenweep National Monument, Utah. Note that, for defense, the two-story, tower-like structure was built on a huge boulder, with very restricted access.

127

(Left) Small Anasazi cliff-dwelling, Horse Canyon, Canyonlands National Park, Utah. (Right) Cave dwelling, Gila Cliff Dwellings National Monument, New Mexico.

(Left) Small granary, Ruin Park, Beef Basin Archaeological Area, Utah. (Right) Doors, Pueblo Bonito ruin, Chaco Canyon National Monument, New Mexico.

Wall details, Chettro Kettle ruins, Chaco Canyon National Monument, New Mexico. Note how ground settling has distorted the big wall.

Anasazi cliff-dwelling, Escalante Canyon, Glen Canyon National Recreation Area, Utah. This ruin has been partially restored and stabilized for public visitation, but can be reached only by boat.

Anasazi ruins, Petrified Forest National Park, Arizona.

Defiance House ruins, Forgotten Canyon, Glen Canyon National Recreation Area, Utah. Part of this cliff-dwelling has been restored and stabilized for public visitation.

Construction details, Betatakin ruin, Navajo National Monument, Arizona.

Dwelling walls and kivas, Aztec Ruins National Monument, New Mexico.

Square Tower House ruins, Mesa Verde National Park, Colorado.

Two-story cave dwelling, Gila Cliff Dwellings National Monument, New Mexico.

(Left) Pueblo Arroyo ruins, Chaco Canyon National Monument, New Mexico.
(Right) Canyon-rim tower, Hovenweep National Monument, Utah.

Walls and beams, Chettro Kettle ruins, Chaco Canyon National Monument, New Mexico.

Canyon-rim dwellings, Hovenweep National Monument, Utah. Note that this structure was built on a sloping rock surface.

Small Fremont cave-dwelling, Aztec Butte, Canyonlands National Park, Utah. Note that the cave roof is supported by two natural rock columns.

(Left) Anasazi cliff-dwelling, upper Salt Creek Canyon, Canyonlands National Park, Utah. (Right) Door detail, Lowry Ruins, Colorado.

(Left) Entrance way to completely restored Great Kiva, Aztec Ruins National Monument, New Mexico. (Right) Detail of Great Kiva, Chettro Kettle ruin, Chaco Canyon National Monument, New Mexico.

(Left) Cave-floor, mud-walled granary, White Canyon, Natural Bridges National Monument, Utah. (Right) Doorways, Pueblo Bonito ruin, Chaco Canyon National Monument, New Mexico.

Multi-storied canyon-rim dwellings, Hovenweep National Monument, Utah.

Restored Anasazi dwelling, Escalante Canyon, Glen Canyon National Recreation Area, Utah. Note that the dwelling has one wall of mortared rock and others of mud-plastered sticks.

Window and wall detail in multi-story Pueblo Bonito ruin, Chaco Canyon National Monument, New Mexico. Note the unusual second-floor corner window.

Cliff-dwelling, Beef Basin Archaeological Area, Utah.

Lowry Ruins, Colorado.

(Left) Doorways, Aztec Ruins National Monument, New Mexico. (Right) Room detail, Chettro Kettle ruin, Chaco Canyon National Monument, New Mexico.

Wall detail, multi-storied dwellings at Pueblo Bonito ruin, Chaco Canyon National Monument, New Mexico.

Cave-dwellings, Gila Cliff Dwellings National Monument, New Mexico.

View from the canyon rim of Chettro Kettle ruins, Chaco Canyon National Monument, New Mexico. Note Great Kiva separate from other structures.

(Left) Doorway detail, unrestored Una Vida ruins, Chaco Canyon National Monument, New Mexico. (Right) Small Anasazi cave dwelling, Beef Basin Archaeological Area, Utah.

Small Anasazi cliff-dwelling, Fish Creek Canyon, Utah.

Small Anasazi cliff-dwelling, Lavender Canyon, Canyonlands National Park, Utah.

Tower Ruins, Horse Canyon, Canyonlands National Park, Utah.

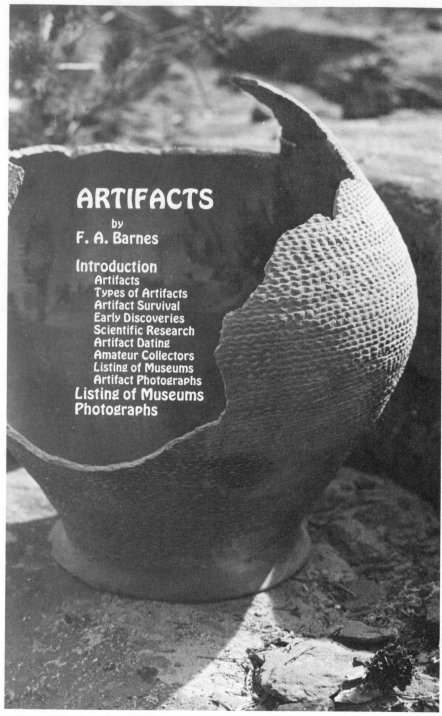

ARTIFACTS
by
F. A. Barnes

Broken Anasazi corrugated pot, Canyonlands National Park collection.

INTRODUCTION

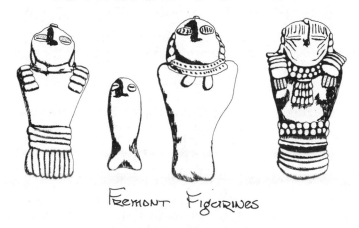

Fremont Figurines

ARTIFACTS

Of the three general categories of surviving remnants of the prehistoric Anasazi and Fremont cultures—the ruins, artifacts and rock art—the artifacts are by far the most important to archaeologists. Although ruins and rock art are, in a way, types of artifacts, they are not nearly as useful to archaeologists who are studying a particular culture as are other less conspicuous types of artifacts.

TYPES OF ARTIFACTS

Ruins are discussed in the preceding chapter and rock art is covered by the following chapter. In addition to these special types of artifacts, there are many others. These can be classified in several ways. In general, artifacts are anything that remains of the prehistoric people themselves, of their possessions, or of anything they changed or affected.

More specifically, the types of artifacts found in the Anasazi and Fremont regions are as follows.

Human remains: consisting of bones, hair, teeth and a few mummies. Most such remains are found in formal burial crypts, but others are found in trash middens and other strange places. Two controversial skeletons were even found, still articulated and apparently *in situ* or "as originally deposited within," a geologic stratum about 135 million years old.

Ceramics: either fired or unfired. These are largely pottery, but also include figurines. Archaeologists also obtain useful information from the remains of fireplaces and kilns, where heat-affected clays and soils are ceramics of a sort.

Basketry: largely of plant products. Such universally used household tools are found throughout the entire region and duration of both Anasazi and Fremont cultures. In fact, the making of baskets is one indicator of an early phase of a distinct cultural subdivision.

Plant fibers: found in woven, twisted or other forms. These may be clothing or other cloth, pads, ropes, nets, snares or the string used for many purposes. Since plant fibers are readily available, even in desert areas, they have also been universally used throughout human prehistory.

Worked stone: again found in many forms because of long, continuous prehistoric use. Common forms are projectile points, such as tips for spears and arrows. Other items made of chipped harder stone include knives, axes, choppers and scrapers. Tools often made from less durable stone are the two parts of grinders, the mortar and pestle, or "metate and mano," the Spanish terms commonly used, plus such worked stone artifacts as "moki steps," or toe-holds cut into stone slopes and cliffs as an aid to climbing, and rocks that were incised, inscribed or grooved for various purposes.

Worked wood: with many and diverse uses. Common uses for wood were structural, for ladders and for tool and weapon shafts. Since wood of varying quality was available everywhere, it was used throughout human prehistory.

Worked animal products: again, widely used in many ways. All fairly durable animal products were used by prehistoric humans for some purpose or another, including hides, hooves, fur, horns, antlers, bones, teeth, claws, feathers and beaks.

Food remnants: such "garbage" as animal bone fragments, cobs, seed hulls, nutshells and fruit husks are valuable artifacts to archaeologists, especially when their exact relationships to other artifacts can be determined using scientific excavation techniques.

Animal bones: of animals that were not used as food. Archaeologists have found that in some areas, certain animals were domesticated or kept as pets, but not used as food. The bones of such animals are thus "artifacts," in the sense that they provide cultural information.

Human feces: as preserved within dry caves. Human waste products can provide very useful information. Properly analyzed, human feces can tell a scientist many things about a prehistoric tribe's diet, diseases, body vermin and even its medical practices.

Other odds and ends: in the Anasazi and Fremont regions, certain artifacts such as sea shells, copper bells, turquoise and obsidian generally came from other cultures, although the fossil shells sometimes used for pendants came from local geologic strata. "Foreign" artifacts are valuable for determining intercultural relationships.

ARTIFACT SURVIVAL

The two principal factors that determined whether a particular artifact survived to the present were the materials that made up the artifact, and where it was abandoned. Some artifacts, such as pottery or items made of stone, could and did survive no matter where they were left by their vanished owners. Others, such as items made of plant fibers, wood, hide and other organic materials, could rarely survive for long unless protected from the elements in a dry cave.

Thus, after hundreds of years, ceramic and stone artifacts have survived virtually unchanged, but artifacts of less resistant materials are relatively rare. Human and animal bones and other durable parts are found many places, but such delicate artifacts as baskets, mummies, clothing, rope, leather and other items made of organic materials are generally found only in dry caves, either within or buried under ruined structures, or buried beneath accumulated layers of dust, sand and other debris.

Illegally excavated Anasazi cave dwelling near Moab, Utah. Vandals have exhumed several human bodies and "collected" the skulls. Although this was reported to the appropriate federal land administration agency, a later visit to the cave revealed that the illegal excavating had continued even after the report.

Of all the prehistoric Anasazi and Fremont artifacts that did survive the elements to modern times, many still disappeared before archaeologists could find and study them. From the moment the first ruins were discovered, such collectable artifacts as pottery, baskets and worked stone weapons and tools were removed from the ruins and squirreled away into private collections, with little or no regard for their scientific value. In many cases, collectors even dug up and took mummies and skulls and other human remains, to sell or to decorate their homes.

Thus, archaeologists have rarely seen canyon country prehistoric ruins, with all the artifacts still where their owners abandoned them. That part of the prehistoric story that could have been revealed by these artifacts that were used during the last days, has been forever obscured by the collectors who systematically stripped the ruins.

EARLY DISCOVERIES

The more obvious and durable artifacts were discovered by early explorers at the same time that structural ruins were found. Newberry, with the 1859 Macomb Expedition, reported ruins, with "pottery scattered about" which was "identical with that before found in so many places."

Major John Wesley Powell reported on July 29, 1869, that while exploring on foot in upper Glen Canyon:

"Just before sundown, I attempt to climb a rounded eminence, from which I hope to obtain a good outlook on the surrounding country. It is formed by smooth mounds, piled one above the other. Up these I climb, winding here and there to find a practicable way, until near the summit they become too steep for me to proceed. I search about a few minutes for an easier way, when I am surprised at finding a stairway, evidently cut into the rock by hands. At one place, where there is a vertical wall of 10 or 12 feet, I find an old rickety ladder. It may be that this was a watchtower of that ancient people whose homes we have found in ruins."

Dellenbaugh, in his report of the 1871 Powell Expedition, also noted finding a prehistoric route out of Labyrinth Canyon on the Green River, where "poles and treetrunks had been placed against the rocks to aid the climbers."

These and other early reports give brief but tantalizing glimpses of what the prehistoric ruins of the Four Corners region were like before they were ravaged by modern collectors and vandals.

SCIENTIFIC RESEARCH

Because so many artifacts were lost to collectors, archaeological research has largely been confined to studying artifacts found during scientific excavations at various sites. Many such excavations have been in connection with the larger prehistoric pueblos, but some have been of earlier dwelling sites or even of large caves that were used for millennia by the Archaic stage predecessors of the Anasazis and Fremonts.

Although most of the artifacts recovered from such scientific "digs" would be scorned by amateur and commercial collectors as "worthless," they are highly valued by archaeologists. Much of this value, however, comes from precisely charting each artifact's location as it is found. Pothunters destroy all such value when they dig into ruins for saleable artifacts.

While many of the earlier "scientific" excavations made in canyon country ruins were little better than licensed vandalism, since the 1920s most archaeological digs in the region have used the best archaeological techniques known at the time. Within recent years, however, much progress has been made in this field, especially in the science of age-dating artifacts.

ARTIFACT DATING

The subject of artifact dating is very complex, and delves into several esoteric branches of the physical sciences. In general, however, dating falls into two categories, relative and absolute.

Relative dating means a technique that enables a researcher to determine the relative ages of various artifacts within a particular site, or a small area. Thus, an archaeologist may know that one human skeleton at a site was buried much earlier than another, but he may still not know when, on our modern calendar, either of them died.

Another relative dating technique may tell a scientist that one obsidian axe was made long after another, but will not tell him exactly when either was made. Among such relative dating techniques are bone-fluorine analysis, obsidian hydration analysis, pollen analysis, and style analysis with pottery and other cultural items. Relating artifact age to such an obvious geologic event as a volcanic eruption is also relative, unless that event can be precisely dated in absolute time.

The scientific value of artifacts that have been relative age-dated is multiplied if that localized relative scale can somehow be tied to our present calendar. There are four major techniques for absolute age-dating now in use. These vary in accuracy, cost, applicability and practicality.

The most accurate, applicable, practical and least expensive, is tree-ring analysis, or *dendrochronology*. If a significant section of a tree trunk can be associated with some part of the relative time scale of an archaeological site, then that entire site can be "connected" to our modern calendar. That is, if it can be stated that the tree used as a dwelling roof beam was cut in a particular year, e.g., 1132 AD, then the relative time scale will help determine the absolute ages of other artifacts at the site. Thus, a tree-trunk roof-beam in a ruin can lead to the accurate dating of almost every artifact found in that ruin and, to a lesser extent, others nearby.

Radiocarbon dating, or C14 dating, is also fairly accurate for recent times, but becomes less accurate further into the past. It also has a practical limit in that it can be applied only to certain types of organic materials that are not always available in ruins. Another technique, based upon the potassium-argon radioactive decay cycle, has even more practical limitations, but is still useful in some cases.

Archeomagnetism involves the fairly accurate dating of fired clays that have not been subsequently moved, such as around prehistoric fireplaces. Despite its limited applicability, this technique is proving to be surprisingly accurate and useful to archaeologists. Even if only one fire site in a whole ruin complex can be dated by this method, that serves to tie that complex to our modern calendar, and hence into the overall cultural pattern.

Another technique for absolute dating that can sometimes be used is to relate known, dated geologic events to some relative archaeological time scale. For example, much may be known about a particular ruin site, but not its exact age on our modern calendar. However, if a nearby volcano erupted sometime during that site's history, and the date of that eruption can be determined with any accuracy, then the ruin can also be dated. Other catastrophic natural events such as floods, earthquakes, mudslides, fires and exceptional freezes can also be used on occasion to help date prehistoric sites and artifacts, and thus increase their usefulness to scientists.

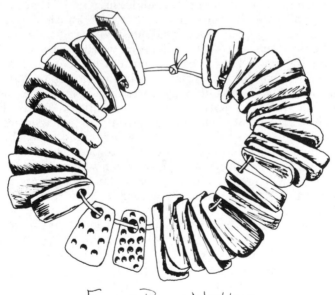

Fremont Bone Necklace

AMATEUR COLLECTORS

For almost a century now, modern commercial collectors and vandals have stripped, dug, ravished and destroyed prehistoric Anasazi and Fremont archaeological sites, taking with them countless thousands of irreplaceable artifacts. In a few places archaeologists have done still more artifact collecting in support of research programs.

Thus, it is highly unlikely that a modern amateur explorer will discover a significant artifact in the canyon country hinterlands. Chipping grounds, where hunters chipped out new points while on a hunt, are fairly common, and an intact arrowhead may still be found occasionally, but for most amateur explorers, the best place to see prehistoric Indian artifacts is in one of the region's many museums.

Most museums have programs that encourage private owners of artifacts to loan their collections for public display. Even though such artifacts lost virtually all scientific value when they were removed from where they were found, displaying them in a museum "on loan" allows the public at least to view prehistoric artifacts that by law actually belong to them. It is hoped by museums that as more private collections go on public display on "long-term loan," the consciences of still other collectors will lead them to share the mystery and antiquity of their artifacts with their rightful owners, the American public.

Present laws and regulations specify that when a prehistoric artifact is found by an amateur explorer, it should be left in place where discovered. Within national and state park areas, and certain other special federal areas, this is enforced, and violators may face fines, imprisonment, or both. On other public lands, while the "no collecting" laws are equally applicable, practical enforcement is severely limited by the lack of funding and by the continued existence of archaic mining laws that permit the unhindered destruction of archaeological sites.

Even now, almost three-quarters of a century after the enactment of the first law protecting this nation's antiquities, Congress has yet to indicate that it really meant what it said in that act by funding its enforcement.

LISTING OF MUSEUMS

All of the museums listed on the following pages are within canyon country or its borderlands, and all have displays of prehistoric Indian artifacts from the Anasazi, Fremont or their neighboring cultures. Some of the displays are quite limited, while others are extensive.

In addition to the museum listed, others at the state universities of the Four Corners states also offer displays of the region's prehistoric Indian artifacts, although these universities are located outside of canyon country. There are also a few U.S. Forest Service visitor centers within the canyon country region that offer displays of artifacts.

Additional small displays of artifacts can also be found throughout canyon country at commercial facilities that sell Indian craft items. Some such facilities even sell prehistoric artifacts, despite the questionable legality of this practice.

By far the greatest numbers of Anasazi and Fremont artifacts are held in private collections or in the dusty warehouses of universities. In either case, the artifacts are not available for public viewing. Some additional artifacts are being held by national and state park officials for later display on a rotational basis, or for display in museums now in the planning stages.

Visitor Center and museum, Gila Cliff Dwellings National Monument, New Mexico.

ARTIFACT PHOTOGRAPHS

All the artifacts depicted in this book are from the Moab Museum, the University of Utah Archaeological Center, or from a Canyonlands National Park collection intended for display at a museum not yet constructed. Appropriate credit is given with each photograph.

The artifacts shown in this book are intended only to be representative. There are far too many types of artifacts, many of them of interest only to archaeologists, to attempt to show more than a few in a book of this size and general nature.

Most of the archaeological reports and books listed under SOURCES, and many of the popular books listed under FURTHER READING, have numerous illustrations showing prehistoric Anasazi and Fremont artifacts.

All artifact photographs in this book are by the author of this chapter unless otherwise credited.

MUSEUMS DISPLAYING PREHISTORIC ARTIFACTS

STATE	MUSEUM NAME OR LOCATION	NEAREST CITIES OR TOWNS	APPROACH HIGHWAYS	COMMENTS
ARIZONA	Grand Canyon National Park	Flagstaff or Williams	U.S. 180 & Arizona 64	Museum is on South Rim, near Desert View, on Arizona 64.
	Petrified Forest National Park	Holbrook or Gallup, N.M.	Interstate 40	Museum displays at both north and south entrances to the park.
	Canyon de Chelly National Monument	Chinle	Arizona 63 & Indian Routes 7 & 64	Displays are at monument visitor center near Chinle.
	Casa Grande Ruins National Monument	Coolidge	Arizona 87	Displays are at monument visitor center.
	Montezuma Castle National Monument	Flagstaff or Camp Verde	Interstate 17	Displays are at monument visitor center.
	Navajo National Monument	Kayenta or Tuba City	U.S. 160 & Arizona 564	Displays are at monument visitor center.
	Tonto National Monument	Globe	U.S. 60 or Arizona 88	Displays are at monument visitor center.
	Tuzigoot National Monument	Jerome or Cottonwood	U.S. 89A	Displays are at monument visitor center.
	Walnut Canyon National Monument	Flagstaff	Interstate 17 or 40 & county road	Displays are at monument visitor center.

153

ARIZONA (continued)	Wupatki National Monument	Flagstaff	U.S. 89	Displays are at monument visitor center.
	Heard Museum	Downtown Phoenix	Interstate 17 or Interstate 10	Permanent collection of southwest cultures.
	Museum of Northern Arizona	Flagstaff	Fort Valley Road, Flagstaff	Museum is open to the public. Inquire locally for directions to the museum.
	Pueblo Grande	Phoenix	Washington St.	Artifacts displayed in Museum.
	Besh Ba Gowah Archaeological Park	Globe	North on U.S. 60	Artifacts displayed at Gila County Museum.
	Kinishba Ruins, Fort Apache Indian Reservation	Whiteriver or Carrizo	Arizona 73	Displays are at nearby Fort Apache, in General Cook's quarters.
	Navajo Tribal Museum	Window Rock	Arizona 264 & Navajo Road 12	Artifacts displayed in Museum.
COLORADO	Mesa Verde National Park	Cortez or Durango	U.S. 160	Displays are at park visitor center.
	Colorado National Monument	Grand Junction or Fruita	Local roads or Interstate 70	Displays are at monument visitor center.
	Anasazi Heritage Center	Cortez	Colorado 184	Artifacts displayed in Museum.
	Crow Canyon Archaeological Center	Cortez	U.S. 666 to County Road L	Self guided tours and displays at center.

NEW MEXICO	Aztec Ruins National Monument	Farmington & Aztec	U.S. 550 & local road	Displays are at monument visitor center.
	Bandelier National Monument	Santa Fe or Española	U.S. 84/285 & New Mexico 4	Displays are at monument visitor center.
	Chaco Canyon National Monument	Bloomfield or Gallup	Interstate 40 & New Mexico 57	Displays are at monument visitor center.
	El Morro National Monument	Gallup or Grants	New Mexico 52 & 53	Displays are at monument visitor center.
	Gila Cliff Dwellings National Monument	Silver City	U.S. 180 & New Mexico 15	Displays are at monument visitor center.
	Gran Quivira National Monument	Carizozo or Mountainair	U.S. 54 & New Mexico 14	Displays are at monument visitor center.
	Pecos National Monument	Santa Fe or Las Vegas	Interstate 25 & New Mexico 63	Displays are at monument visitor center.
	Coronado State Monument	Albuquerque & Bernalillo	U.S. 85 or Interstate 25 & New Mexico 44	Displays are at monument visitor center.
	Jemez State Monument	Jemez Springs	New Mexico 4	Displays are at monument museum.
	Quarai State Monument	Mountainair	U.S. 60	Displays are at monument museum.
	Maxwell Museum of Anthropology, UNM	Albuquerque	U.S. 66	Permanent and rotating exhibits.

UTAH			
Arches National Park	Moab	U.S. 191	Displays are at park visitor center.
Bryce Canyon National Park	Panguitch	U.S. 89 & Utah 12 & 63	Displays are at museum near park entrance.
Capitol Reef National Park	Torrey & Hanksville	Utah 24	Displays are at park visitor center.
Zion National Park	Springdale or Kanab	Utah 15 & U.S. 89	Displays are at park visitor center.
Dinosaur National Monument	Vernal & Jensen	U.S. 40 & Utah 149	Displays are at monument visitor center.
Hovenweep National Monument	Blanding or Bluff	U.S. 191, Utah 262 & county road	Displays are at monument visitor center.
Natural Bridges National Monument	Blanding or Hanksville	U.S. 191, Utah 95 & 275	Displays are at monument visitor center.
Flaming Gorge National Recreation Area	Vernal, or Green River, WY	Utah 44 & 43 & Wyoming 530	Displays are at Red Canyon visitor center.
Anasazi Indian Village State Historical Monument	Boulder	Utah 12	Displays are at monument visitor center.
Edge of Cedars State Historical Monument	Blanding	U.S. 191 & city-county roads	Displays are at museum. Follow signs from U.S. 191 in Blanding.
College of Eastern Utah Prehistoric Museum	Price	U.S. 50 & 6	Permanent and rotating exhibits.

UTAH (continued)			
Dead Horse Point State Park	Moab	U.S. 191 & Utah 313	Displays are at park visitor center.
Dinosaur Natural History Museum	Vernal	U.S. 40	Museum is on U.S. 40 just east of town center.
Fremont State Park	Richfield	I-70 Clear Creek Canyon Exit	Artifacts displayed in Museum.
Utah Field House of Natural History State Park	Vernal	U.S. 40	Artifacts displayed in Museum.
Monticello Library & Museum	Monticello	U.S. 191	Displays are in basement of library, center of town.
Moab Museum	Moab	U.S. 191	Museum is one block east of U.S. 191 on Center St.
Navajo Tribal Park, Monument Valley	Mexican Hat & Kayenta, AZ	U.S. 191 & dirt road	Displays are at visitor center, 4 miles from U.S. 191.

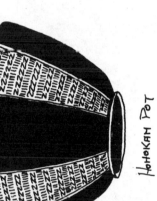

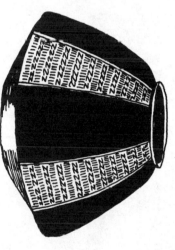

Hohokam Pot

Very small pitcher.

Artifacts on this and the following twelve pages are from the Moab Museum collection except as otherwise noted. Photos by F.A. Barnes.

Bowl

Seashell necklace

Unwoven yucca fibers, twine and basket, Moab Museum collection.

(Left) Grooved rocks below Five Faces pictographs at an Anasazi ceremonial site, Davis Canyon, Canyonlands National Park, Utah. (Right) Grooved rocks at an Anasazi ceremonial site, purpose uncertain but probably for grinding plant products used in planting, growing or harvesting ceremonies.

Anasazi skull

Two ceramic ladles

Stone ax heads and pot

Anasazi pot

Broken jar, probably Anasazi

Arrow and spear points

Miscellaneous small items

Bowl

Shallow ceramic bowl. Note the holes around the bowl's rim, which may have been used to attach woven basketry.

Small pitchers, probably Anasazi

Mortar and pestle

Wooden tools

Wood-handled knife and sheep's horn paint pot

Pottery ladle

(Left) Visitor center and museum, Capitol Reef National Park, Utah. (Right) Woven basket and sandal, probably Anasazi.

(Left) Anasazi pot. (Right) Tiny animal made of reeds, probably an Anasazi toy.

Stone ax heads

Pots

Bowl

Tightly-woven tray, corn cobs and tiny ceramic object

(Left) Visitor center and museum, Aztec Ruins National Monument, New Mexico.
(Right) Small fire-blackened pot.

Large bowl, probably Anasazi

Miscellaneous stone items and seashell. Seashells were trade items

Painted gourd

(Left) Leather sandals, Moab Museum collection. (Right) Wooden tools, Canyonlands National Park collection.

170

Miscellaneous points

Artifacts on this and the following six pages are from the Canyonlands National Park collection except as otherwise noted. Photos by F.A. Barnes.

Wooden and bone tools

Woven sandals

Broken Anasazi pot

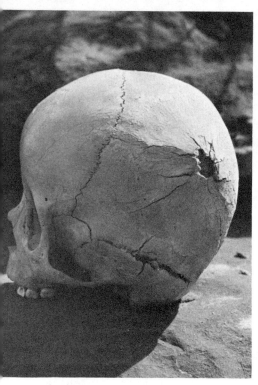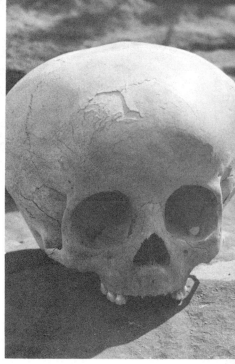

Front and side view of Anasazi child's skull, showing probably cause of death. Canyonlands National Park collection.

172

Tiny inch-high ram's head carved from horn

Large broken jar

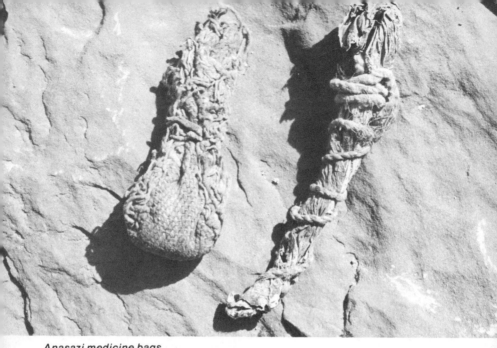

Anasazi medicine bags

Large broken spearhead

Tightly-woven sandal

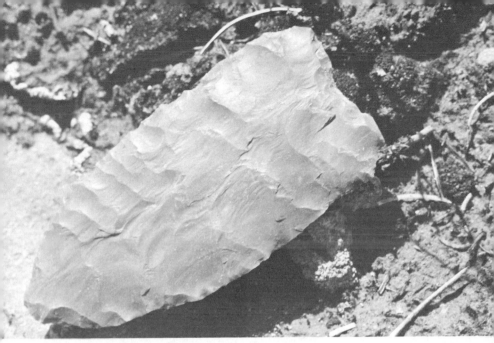

Large Anasazi spearhead

(Left) Anasazi bows. (Right) Large two-hand grinding stone and smaller stone tool.

175

Bone awls

Illegal excavation in Anasazi cave dwelling near Moab, Utah, showing exhumed human bones.

Large corrugated Anasazi pot

Anasazi bowl

Artifacts on this and the following four pages are from the University of Utah Archaeological Center collection.

Anasazi pitcher

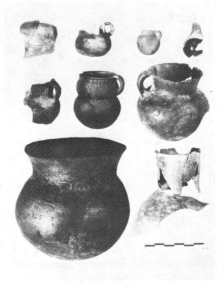

Various Fremont ceramics

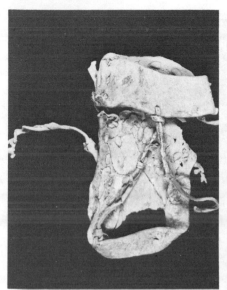 

(Left) Leather Fremont sandal. (Right) Anasazi jar, pieced together from fragments.

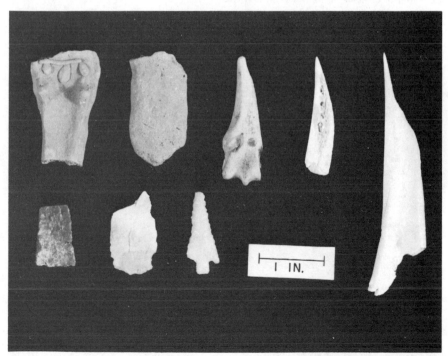

I IN.

Miscellaneous Anasazi artifacts of stone, bone and clay

179

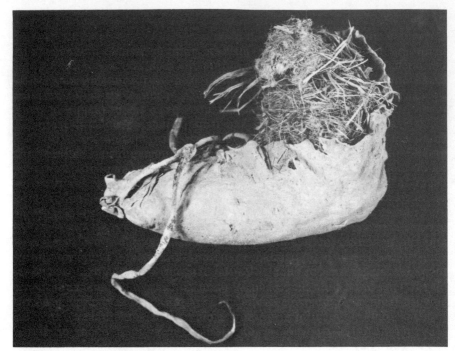

Leather pouch or child's moccasin, Fremont

Fremont manos, or grinding stones

Corrugated Anasazi pot

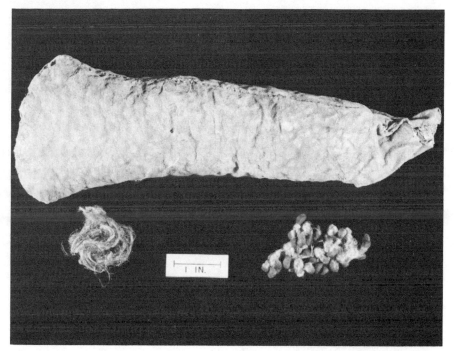

Anasazi leather seed bag

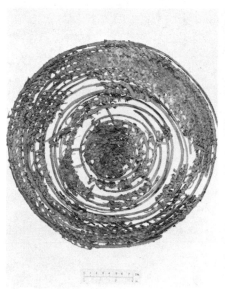

Fragments of Anasazi basket

Anasazi corrugated jar

181

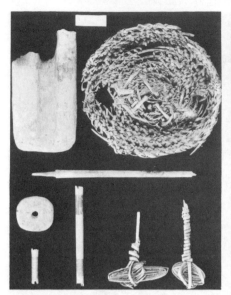
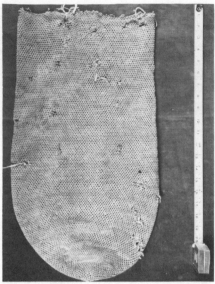

(Left) Miscellaneous Anasazi artifacts of wood and fiber. (Right) Twined cordage bag. This large Fremont bag contained a number of items when found.

Anasazi jar

ROCK ART
by
F. A. Barnes

Introduction
Definition
Methods and Materials
Locations
Subject Matter
The Artists
Early Reports
Archaeological Reports
Rock Art Dating
Rock Art Styles
Interpretation
Listing of Rock Art Sites
Rock Art Photographs
Listing of Rock Art Sites
Photographs

Fremont petroglyph, Sego Canyon, Utah.

INTRODUCTION

Fremont Rock Art

DEFINITIONS

The prehistoric Amerind rock art of the general Four Corners region is fascinating, mystifying, challenging and aesthetically pleasing to canyon country visitors, yet to archaeologists it is the most baffling, enigmatic, controversial and neglected of all artifacts.

Defined narrowly, "rock art" would be limited to prehistoric scribblings on rock that were intended to be "art," a definition that would raise many questions. Defined more broadly, "rock art" would mean any kind of markings made on almost any kind of durable surface, by any means, of any subject and for any purpose, but excluding pottery, which can be treated separately even though there is a relationship between pottery designs and rock art designs within the same locale.

Within this broad definition of "rock art" there are two general classes, "petroglyphs" and "pictographs." Other terms are also used, even by some archaeologists, but these two terms are now standard within the field of archaeology, and between them cover all the various kinds of rock art that exist. These two terms are self-defining, while other terms sometimes used are confusing and non-definitive.

"Petroglyph" is a composite word meaning "rock marking," that is, some kind of image or design cut into a rock surface, without any use of pigment or coloring.

"Pictograph" means "picture," or "painted image," implying the use of pigments to create an image upon rock or some other surface, without cutting into that surface.

There are, of course, a few examples of rock art that defy even these standard definitions, where both cutting and painting techniques were used to produce an image, but these are fairly rare in canyon country.

METHODS AND MATERIALS

Petroglyphs were produced by either pecking, scratching or scraping the desired image into the surface of one rock, using another usually harder rock as a tool. In canyon country, the rock surface most commonly used was sandstone darkened with "desert varnish." This brown or black rock coloration builds up on rocks in desert areas after prolonged exposure, if the rocks contain certain minerals.

Brown desert varnish is an iron oxide, and can occur only if the rock contains enough iron in some form or another. Since the reddish hue that occurs in many canyon country sandstone formations comes from an iron mineral, brown desert varnish is common in the region.

Black desert varnish is a manganese oxide. Since traces of manganese occur within many canyon country rock formations, this type of desert varnish is also common. Some of the darker patinas found on the region's sandstone surfaces are, of course, combinations of iron and manganese oxides.

The complex chemistry of desert varnish formation is not entirely understood. It is a very slow process that involves internal minerals and moisture, the hot desert sun, and a series of chemical reactions within the rock and on its surface. Surface moisture also affects the formation of brown desert varnish. This can be seen where sandstone walls exhibit beautiful "draperies" of varnish in patterns created by rain runoff. The formation of black desert varnish seems to be less affected by surface moisture. Most of the blackening seen in rain runoff patterns on cliffs is from dark colored lichens and other micro-plants growing on the rock surface, not from black desert varnish.

In general, the darker a desert varnish — whether brown or black or a mixture — the longer that surface has been exposed, although there are exceptions to this. A rock surface can be exposed for a very long time, yet have no surface patina of varnish if the basic conditions of mineral content, moisture and sunshine are not all present.

Canyon country prehistoric Indians were not concerned with these technicalities, however. They simply took advantage of the fact that, if the desert varnish on a rock surface was somehow removed, a satisfying image was produced by the color contrast between the remaining varnish and the lighter-hued rock revealed. Thus, almost all petroglyphs in canyon country are found on sandstone surfaces that have been darkened by desert varnish.

In general, anything that would remove the desert varnish in the desired pattern could be used by the petroglyph "artist." In practice, however, since canyon country Indians were still "stone age," that is, they had no metals, the commonest tool used to produce petroglyphs was a piece of harder rock, such as the agate, chert or jasper common to the region.

Techniques varied, but included pecking away the desert varnish with repeated blows; scratching repeatedly along lines with a sharp

Anasazi petroglyphs in dark desert varnish, San Juan River gorge, Utah.

Anasazi pictographs, upper Salt Creek Canyon, Canyonlands National Park, Utah.

186

edge; scraping or abrading away an area of varnish with a rubbing motion; or drilling small holes in patterns, using wooden drill rods tipped with harder stone. A few petroglyphs were even enhanced by the addition of colored pigments to the pattern of raw rock revealed by the varnish removal.

In contrast, pictographs were usually painted on rock surfaces that were light-colored and relatively free of desert varnish. In general, pictograph "artists" also chose surfaces that were fairly firm, smooth and free of defects, although not all canyon country rock-artists were so discriminating.

Pictographs were painted with pigments made from locally available mineral deposits, or from charcoal made from burned wood or other plant materials. Such mineral deposits usually occur as soft, thin layers of colorful minerals that can be used directly by wetting them, or by grinding them up and then applying them in a thick fluid suspension. Some pictographs have been observed that were obviously made by the simple expedient of rubbing a wetted finger along a seam of colorful clay, then using the finger to paint the image on a nearby rock wall.

It is possible that some pictographs were painted with pigments or stains from an organic source, such as plant juices or even blood, but if so, such paints have long since decayed and disappeared. Mineral pigments are far more resistant to the ravages of time and the elements than organic pigments.

The techniques used by prehistoric pictograph artists for producing their images no doubt varied just as widely as they do among modern artists, but in general, the paint was applied either by using the fingers or fabricated brushes, or by blowing the paint through a hollow reed onto the rock surface. This primitive "spray gun" technique was often used to create "negative images," by spraying around a hand held against the rock surface.

Negative-image hand pictographs, Fish Creek Canyon, Utah.

187

Many petroglyphs and pictographs are essentially line drawings, that is, they consist of images created by combinations of straight or curved lines of varying widths, with little or no shading or filling in of areas. At some sites, however, the rock-artists have gone to considerable trouble to fill in their images, either by pecking or scraping if the image is a petroglyph, or by painting in the outlined pictograph image. A few pictograph images are all fill, without any discernible contrasting outline.

Petroglyphs and pictographs vary widely in size, with the artist's whims apparently being the guiding factor. Most petroglyphs vary from small to medium sized, with the crude nature of the inscribing process imposing a lower limit to size. Virtually all petroglyphs depicting humans or animals are smaller than life size.

Conversely, the relative ease with which paint can be applied has led to many pictographs in which humans or animals are shown full scale or even larger. As with petroglyphs, the pictograph paint-on-rock medium imposes a limitation on size but, even so, there are many quite detailed small pictographs.

LOCATIONS

The prehistoric Indians who created canyon country rock art were well aware that petroglyphs were quite durable when exposed to the elements, and that their painted pictographs were not. It would be very difficult to prove that these stone-age artists were concerned over whether their graphics would endure down through the centuries, for the edification or mystification of future generations or alien cultures, but it would be safe to assume that they wanted their efforts to last at least for their lifetimes.

With petroglyphs, this was no problem. They could be located almost anywhere, except on rock so weathered or poorly petrified that it was crumbling away. Even if there were no desert varnish to provide color contrast, or if new varnish gradually darkened the 'glyph, its impression in the rock would still endure.

Pictographs, however, were another matter. Rain, wind and direct sunlight could erode or fade pictograph paint pigments, and high humidity could cause the paint, or the stone beneath the pictograph, to scale away, destroying it completely. Apparently, pictograph artists were aware of this, because virtually all known pictograph panels are in locations that protect them from the elements. It is conceivable, of course, that pictograph artists simply ignored the elements, and that only pictographs in sheltered locations survived to the present, but this is not likely.

Whatever the cause, pictographs are now found only in protected locations, although the deteriorated condition of some indicates their sites were poorly chosen. Pictographs are generally found on smooth, light-colored sandstone walls within caves or alcoves, or beneath overhanging ledges or cliffs. At a few sites, rock collapses have reduced such overhead protection, or have even carried away whole sections of pictograph panels.

Very faded and eroded pictographs in a cave between Hellroaring and Spring canyons, Utah. Probably Fremont culture.

Pictographs — whether a few figures or a huge panel of many figures — may be located at a habitation area or some nearby site, or remote from any apparent usage area. A few pictographs also occur on the surviving mud-plastered walls of ruins. There may have been many more that did not survive to the present. Archaeologists believe that there may be a relationship between pictograph panel locations and the meanings or usages of the pictographs, but these scientists are not yet ready to describe such relationships in detail.

Petroglyphs, being quite durable and requiring no special skills or materials to make, are much more common than pictographs, and occur in a wide variety of locations. They do, however, seem to be found more often in certain types of locations, such as near dwellings, along game trails, near springs and streams, near hunting or foraging camps, or at key points along commonly used travel routes.

At such sites, the 'glyphs are usually located on cliff walls or large, detached boulders, whose surfaces have been darkened with desert varnish. Some sites show evidence of many different artists, over long stretches of time, and even from different cultures. It is not uncommon in canyon country to find a petroglyph site with 'glyphs made by prehistoric Indians, historic Indians, early pioneers and cattlemen, and contemporary vandals.

In addition to those found on cliffs and large boulders, petroglyphs also appear on two other types of rocks. In a few locations, 'glyphs have been found on smaller boulders set at intervals around open dwelling sites. It is easy to conclude that these marked boulders had a meaning, such as "this is my land—trespass at your own risk," or "plague—keep out," or "taboo—sacred ground," but this has not been proven.

Petroglyphs have also been discovered in the form of strange markings and patterns scratched onto small rocks. Most of such rocks found within canyon country to date have come from cave excavations, but similar artifacts have also been found in Nevada and California.

Three factors have contributed to the long-range preservation of prehistoric canyon country rock art, from its creation over the past several thousand years to the present. One factor has been the durable nature of petroglyphs and the mineral pigments that were used in most pictographs.

The second factor has been the locations of rock art sites in protected caves, and on the faces of cliffs and large boulders, and the widespread distribution of rock art sites throughout the terribly rough and broken canyon country hinterlands. The location of rock art on the faces of cliffs and huge boulders has also protected most of it, but not all, from destructive mineral search and development activities. Not even bulldozers can destroy cliffs. It takes explosives.

The third factor that has served to protect canyon country rock art, at least from total destruction if not vandalism, is again due to its location on cliff faces and huge boulders. In some western regions, rock art occurs on small rock masses and boulders that private and commercial collectors can steal from public land, but the cliffs and huge boulders of canyon country are virtually impossible to collect. This has left this region's invaluable legacy of prehistoric rock art still largely intact, although badly marred by graffiti in locations that are easily accessible to the public and unprotected by ranger surveillance.

Most of the vandalism that has defaced many spectacular canyon country rock art panels has been either the thoughtless, egocentric addition of names, initials and dates to the panels, or simple, mindless destruction or defacement, using metal tools, paint or bullets. Some defacement, however, has been by people who should know better, such as archaeologists and artists.

Archaeologists have been known to apply paint and permanent markings to magnificently beautiful pictograph panels, simply for the sake of convenient measurement. Both archaeologists and photographers quite commonly apply chalk and other marking materials to both petroglyphs and pictographs to make them photograph better, and artists have been known to apply strange chemical mixtures to petroglyphs in order to transfer the images onto cloth or paper or metal foil.

While their locations and durability have protected most petroglyphs and pictographs from natural and human destruction, a few

Petroglyphs in the Colorado River gorge beside Utah 279. Note the white substance left on one 'glyph by someone attempting to reproduce it. Such defacement is just as illegal as outright vandalism.

have nonetheless suffered from natural events. Massive rockfalls from the faces of cliffs have partially destroyed some lovely panels of rock art. Two examples of such destruction are the principal rock art display beside Utah 24 in the Fremont River gorge in Capitol Reef National Park, and the main pictograph panel in the Horseshoe Canyon annex of Canyonlands National Park. At each site, parts of figures still remain as mute testimony to nature's indifference to man's puny creations.

At other locations, the slow but constant scaling away of rock surfaces has taken its toll on rock art. One such site can be seen beside the paved road that branches west from Utah 24 near Goblin Valley State Park, to enter the San Rafael Swell through Temple Mountain Wash. The scaling pictograph panel is within sight of the road where the wash narrows between yellowish sandstone walls.

Fremont pictographs, Temple Wash in the San Rafael Swell, Utah. Note how the scaling rock is slowly destroying the images.

191

SUBJECT MATTER

The subject matter of canyon country prehistoric rock art is quite diverse, but can be classified into five, possibly six, general categories. Of these, the first and most common category is human figures, or "anthropomorphs." These may vary from simple hand or foot outlines, to crude stick figures, to bodies shaped like rectangles or triangles with equally crude heads and limbs or no limbs at all, to quite elaborate full figures or separate heads.

A second major category is animals, or "zoomorphs." Of these, the common game animals such as deer and desert sheep dominate, but other wild animals appear too, such as cats, bears, snakes, foxes, coyotes, bison, birds and occasionally fish, as well as animals that were kept as pets, such as dogs and, in some areas, turkeys and parrots.

The third category is geometric patterns, such as squares, triangles, circles, dots, spirals and other more complex figures, sometimes repeated in rows or larger patterns, or filled in with other geometric designs. The variety of such geometric rock art is endless.

The fourth category is groupings of lines that appear to represent some major aspect of the natural terrain, such as rivers, streams, mountains or canyons. Whether or not a particular image falls into this category is, of course, a matter for conjecture. Very few so obviously represent local geographic features that they are beyond any other interpretation.

The fifth category could be labeled "who knows?" Unfortunately, a considerable amount of rock art falls into this class, some of it simply because it was very crudely done or was not completed, but most of it appearing to be nothing more than random prehistoric doodling, by very unskilled doodlers who had nothing specific in mind, or who were more concerned with technique than content. Then, as now, the means, opportunity and urge do not necessarily produce an artist, no matter how broadly the term may be defined.

The possible sixth category is supernatural entities. Although there is no way to prove beyond doubt that certain human-like figures were supposed to be supernatural beings, some experts are convinced that at certain sites, some or all of the anthropomorphic figures represent supernatural beings such as spirits or gods.

THE ARTISTS

Any detailed discussion concerning the prehistoric "artists" who created canyon country rock art would become hopelessly entangled with other aspects of rock art study, such as its age, meaning and original use. In general, however, canyon country rock art was produced by the two cultures that dominated the region, the Anasazis and the Fremonts.

Exotic Fremont petroglyph figure, Ninemile Canyon, Utah. This figure was obviously not intended to depict a human or animal, but may have represented a demon, god or spirit.

Fremont rock art, however, is not found only within the Fremont cultural territory, nor is Anasazi rock art confined to the region once dominated by the Anasazis. The individuals within each culture who created rock art were evidently quite mobile, some no doubt because they were members of hunting or foraging parties. There may have been other travelers, however, whose sole purpose was to place rock art images at key locations, for specific reasons.

It is thus quite likely that, for whatever reasons, there was within each prehistoric culture a small group of individuals who created the "important" rock art; a much larger category of individuals who were permitted to make certain types of less important images; and all the rest, who were specifically prohibited from making rock art images.

It is highly probable that this last group included all children and most women—otherwise every rock wall near every dwelling site would have been covered with rock art grafitti. In fact, many dwelling sites are entirely free of rock art, indicating a powerful taboo of some sort. Some women, of course, were responsible for the graphic designs on the pottery, and archaeologists have noticed relationships between these designs and some of the geometric patterns that appear in rock art, but there is little indication that these two groups of images were produced by the same individuals. It is more probable that pottery art work was women's business, while the more meaningful and important rock art was the business of men, and not all men, at that.

If such a "division of labor" did in fact exist, there is some evidence that the taboos were not always rigidly enforced. Child-sized handprints are found many places. And, as noted earlier, some rock art seems to have been done by very unskilled hands. These few exceptions, however, seem to reinforce more than refute the concept of a very limited number of rock "artists."

Historic rock art, Arches National Park, Utah.

Not all canyon country rock art is Anasazi or Fremont, however. As noted earlier, subsequent cultures have all too often added their marks to panels of prehistoric art. A few such additions were made by nomadic prehistoric Indians who entered the region, either before or after the Anasazis and Fremonts occupied it. Others were added by such historic and contemporary tribes as the Navajos, Paiutes, and Utes. The cultural origin of one outstanding site—the pictograph

194

panels in the Horseshoe Canyon annex of Canyonlands National Park—has yet to be positively determined. Rock art experts contend that it is neither Anasazi nor Fremont, even though it closely resembles the latter.

Later, Spanish explorers and military parties added their marks to a few rock art locations, and pioneering Americans seemed impelled to prove their existence—and minimal literary capabilities—by scratching their names and dates on rock art panels. The cattlemen and miners who followed the pioneers continued this practice, as have all too many individuals from our modern American culture.

Very little canyon country rock art known to predate the Anasazi and Fremont cultures has been positively identified. Only a few scribed rocks found in cave-excavation strata that could be age-dated have been proven to be from the pre-Formative, Archaic stage culture. One such rock is 8700 years old.

EARLY REPORTS

There is no doubt that early Spanish, Mexican and American exploring and military expeditions saw samples of canyon country prehistoric rock art. At El Morro, a huge sandstone promontory in New Mexico, historic names and dates have been inscribed near prehistoric petroglyphs. The earliest Spanish date is 1605 A.D. Mexican and American dates are more recent, but written reports of these and the other petroglyphs that must have been seen by these early canyon country visitors, are virtually nonexistent.

The first known written reports that mention the prehistoric rock art of the general Four Corners region are dated 1852 and 1855. The first was by a military survey expedition, which noted some rock art near the present town of Manti, Utah, and included sketches. The second was in the diary of a member of the first Mormon mission to settle at the present site of Moab, Utah.

Major John Wesley Powell, on his 1869 expedition down the Green and Colorado rivers, reported finding prehistoric rock art in upper Glen Canyon where, near a ruin, "on the face of the cliff, under the building and along down the river for 200 or 300 yards, there are many etchings." Dellenbaugh, who documented Powell's 1871 explorations, also reported rock art sites in the region.

In the late 1800s and early 1900s, several other exploring and scientific expeditions reported finding rock art, but most such reports treated the subject very lightly. Some who must have seen rock art did not even mention it.

Historic Spanish inscription above prehistoric petroglyphs, El Morro National Monument, New Mexico.

ARCHAEOLOGICAL REPORTS

Beginning about 1920, archaeological reports about Four Corners region prehistory began to mention the rock art there, but very few archaeologists took the subject seriously or attempted to study it in depth. Although there are now more archaeologists investigating rock art than ever before, their numbers are still too few, possibly because the subject is bafflingly complex, and very difficult to integrate with the main body of cultural knowledge.

Today, there are several scientific reports and books available on the subject of canyon country prehistoric rock art, some by archaeologists who are pioneering in this difficult specialty. But these books largely describe and classify the rock art at various sites, with analysis being minimal. In each case, the authors admit that a great deal more study is needed before knowledge of rock art is on a par with what is known about other aspects of the Anasazi and Fremont cultures. Many of the archaeological reports that give only superficial attention to rock art, are guilty of making very unscientific conjectures and assumptions about the subject, and of jumping to conclusions unsupported by the data then on hand.

In sum, the scientific study of canyon country rock art is just beginning, and most statements made concerning the age, purpose and meaning of this special type of prehistoric artifact must be considered working hypotheses, not firm conclusions backed by plenty of research data.

ROCK ART DATING

Rock art cannot be dated accurately by any technique presently known. This makes it virtually impossible to associate rock art with other cultural factors with any certainty. This has long discouraged most archaeologists from pursuing any serious investigation of rock art. The subject is simply too isolated and baffling and elusive; too unrewarding, professionally; and too frustrating, personally.

Upon first examination, the problem of rock art dating does not seem so difficult. Surely, the pictographs in a cave that contains ruins are the same age as the ruins. But are they? And what is the age of the ruins? Using three of the most useful dating methods — dendrochronology, radiocarbon and archeomagnetism — a thorough investigation of the cave may show that it was occupied from, say, 805 to 1317 A.D. When, then, within this 512 year span were the pictographs made, and where is there any direct evidence that they were not put there before or since the period of occupancy?

It is thus obvious that even in this "best case" situation, rock art cannot be dated even roughly with any assurance, and in most cases, such as when the rock art is not near or associated with any other prehistoric cultural artifacts, such dating-by-association is at best an educated guess. Even the inscribed smaller rock noted earlier, that was dated from the cave stratum in which it was found, was dated by associated materials, with only a fair probability that this association was correct.

However, since the usual dating methods simply will not work on rock art, archaeologists use this association method wherever possible, despite its inaccuracy and uncertainty. They call it "dating by inference," and there are several means by which such rough dating can be done.

One is by relating rock art to dated pottery artifacts. Since ceramics are quite durable, and potsherds are in abundant supply in ruins throughout the region, archaeologists have accumulated an enormous body of knowledge about pottery designs, styles, decorations and uses in relation to cultures, subcultures and local customs. This knowledge has been firmly connected with the cultural calendar shown on the inside back cover.

Thus, by inference, by associating certain rock art with seemingly related ceramic designs and decorations, that rock art can be assigned a tentative date, and by secondary inference, all rock art of the same

Pictographs above Defiance House ruins, Forgotten Canyon, Glen Canyon National Recreation Area, Utah.

graphic style can be assigned to the same time period. Again, such primary and secondary inferences, or associations, are not the neat scientific work most archaeologists prefer, and are of questionable accuracy at best, but as more and more such inferences point to the same conclusion, the probability that the conclusion is correct becomes greater and greater.

Associating rock art with datable dwellings or other structures has been noted earlier. In a very few instances, where pictographs occur on the plastered walls of a structure, the art work can be accurately associated with the erection date of the structure. There are still minor variables even then, such as how long was it between the cutting of the roof beam and its use? How many years passed after the basic structure was built before it was mud-plastered? And how long after that before the pictograph was applied; and was it painted over the original plaster, or over a subsequent layer applied fifty years later?

Detailed analyses of rock art graphic styles, techniques and contents have led to several classification systems. These can be used, again by inference, to place individual rock art images into general time brackets. For example, a particular petroglyph might be classified as "late Pueblo III," and thus dated at 1250 to 1300 A.D.

There are still other methods for dating rock art by inference, and no doubt new methods will be devised as research into this elusive archaeological specialty continues. There are also two other general approaches to rock art dating that have some value, although they are still less precise than the inference approach.

One approach is much like that used to apply a relative time scale to the various artifacts within a ruin complex; but with rock art, relative time scales are only vague approximations. Even so, they can be useful to archaeologists.

The ages of various petroglyphs and pictographs in relationship to each other, and to other prehistoric artifacts in the vicinity, can be determined by a number of methods, some of them fairly reliable, others hardly better than guesswork. Then, as noted earlier, the value of any information set on a relative time scale can be increased by relating that scale to an absolute scale such as our modern calendar.

Among the many techniques used to establish the relative ages of petroglyphs, pictographs and other more datable artifacts are the following:

Severely weathered Anasazi petroglyphs, San Juan River gorge, Utah.

Desert varnish slowly builds up within petroglyphs. Thus, on a particular petroglyph panel, the darker the build-up, the older the petroglyph. This rule cannot, however, be applied with any certainty to different panels, because the rates of desert varnish formation vary drastically. The erosion of exposed rock surfaces by wind and water can sometimes give clues to the relative ages of petroglyphs but, again, not with much certainty because of varying erosion rates.

On the same panel, pictographs with the least deterioration, or scaling away, are probably the newest. This rule does not apply to pictographs in different locations, however, because the rate of exfoliation of rock surfaces depends upon many factors.

Again, on the same panel, the relative ages of the various images can sometimes be determined by overlap. For example, if a petroglyph of a bear overlaps and partly obliterates a desert sheep petroglyph, the bear 'glyph is obviously the younger of the two; is probably younger than all other sheep on the panel, and may even be younger than all other 'glyphs done in the same style as the sheep, not only on this panel but on others, too.

Petroglyph panel, Colorado River gorge, beside Utah 279. Note how the bear 'glyph has been superimposed over an older scene in which hunters use bows to attack a herd of desert sheep. The large size of this scene can be determined by comparison with the numerous bullet holes in it. Vandals with guns are especially destructive because they can damage rock art that is otherwise inaccessible.

Rock art images can help establish relative time scales, and even connections with the modern calendar. For example, a petroglyph of a hunter with bow and arrow means that the petroglyph was made since the bow came into use, a point in time that can be established by various means for particular regions or cultures. *Atlatls* are also keys to the time factor when they appear in rock art, as are many other objects depicted.

Rock art graphic techniques also give clues to relative ages between rock art figures, and between rock art and other cultural factors. Careful study has permitted a few archaeologists to classify most rock art by artistic-style-plus-content. This approach has its limits, however, because sophistication of the rock art style and the degree of cultural advancement did not always coincide. For example, the relatively backward Fremont culture produced rock art far more complex than that produced by the Anasazis. In fact, at Mesa Verde and Chaco Canyon, two of the most advanced centers of the Anasazi culture, the rock art is amazingly poor and scarce, while in some of the least developed Fremont regions there are magnificent panels of petroglyphs and pictographs, done in highly sophisticated styles.

The second general approach to the relative age-dating of rock art could be called the "point in time." As noted with the bow and *atlatl*, certain subjects help establish dates of the "not before" type. Most of these deal with rock art created since the cultural heyday of the Anasazis and Fremonts, the exceptions being key tools or weapons developed during the Archaic or early Formative periods. For example, rock art showing horses must date since the Spanish first started exploring canyon country in the early 1600s A.D. because, before then, there were no modern horses on this continent. Rock art showing guns, hats and other European innovations is similarly dated. Rock art showing Navajo, Ute or Paiute subject matter or designs also dates itself, because considerable is known about these tribes, from prehistoric times to the present.

Oddly, lichens can also sometimes give clues to petroglyph age, if they occur on the 'glyphs. Although lichen growth rates vary with such factors as species, moisture, sunlight and mineral content of the rock, the growth is very slow, at best. Thus, some archaeologists use a rule of thumb—that if a petroglyph has lichens within the markings, the 'glyph is probably more than 600 years old. Exceptions to this rule have been observed, however.

Certain apparent anomalies among rock art figures tend to confuse the age-dating process. One such anomaly is caused by the tendency of a few Navajos to "touch-up" or improve authentic prehistoric rock art by re-pecking the petroglyphs, or re-painting the pictographs. In either case, the ancient rock art takes on a "recent" appearance, even though it may be a thousand years old.

Another anomalous factor is the occurrence of animal rock art images, where the animals shown are either long extinct, do not resemble animals known to have been contemporaneous with prehistoric Amerinds, or were not even contemporaneous with the human race. Several examples will illustrate the confusion created by such odd rock art creatures.

There is a petroglyph in Natural Bridges National Monument that bears a startling resemblance to a dinosaur, specifically a Brontosaurus, with long tail and neck, small head and all.

In the San Rafael Swell, there is a pictograph that looks very much like a pterosaur, a Cretaceous flying reptile. The artists who created this "pterosaur," and the "dinosaur," could, of course, have been trying to portray some other real or imagined creatures. But what about other animals seen on rock art panels, such as "impalas," "ostriches," "mammoths" and others that either are long extinct in the western hemisphere, or were never here at all?

Such anomalous rock art figures can be explained away, but they still tend to cast doubt upon the admittedly flimsy relative-time age-dating schemes used by archaeologists. The "impalas" and "ostriches," as with the "dinosaur" and "pterosaur," could simply be poor artistry, or artistic imagination. But how to explain an elephant-like creature, including the long, prehensile trunk?

"Mammoth" petroglyph, Colorado River gorge, near Moab, Utah. Since this photograph was taken, several more bullet holes have badly damaged this controversial 'glyph.

There are two such "mammoths" near Moab, Utah. One is a short distance downriver from Moab Valley, in the Colorado River gorge. The other is in Indian Creek Canyon, within sight of Utah 211 as that highway travels from U.S. 163 to the Needles district of Canyonlands National Park. There are interesting arguments on both sides of the historic-or-prehistoric controversy that centers on these two petroglyphs.

On the "prehistoric" side, neither petroglyph appears to be recent. Both have desert varnish built up within the chipped-out parts of the 'glyphs. Further, it is widely accepted by anthropologists and paleontologists that early Amerinds hunted such large mammals as giant bison, mammoths and giant sloths, and may even have brought about their extinction.

On the "historic" side, the two "mammoth" petroglyphs do not appear to be much older, if any, than the many other 'glyphs nearby, 'glyphs that are clearly associated with the most recent stages of prehistoric cultures that did not even exist 2000 years ago. Paleontologists estimate that mammoths went extinct on this continent about 10,000 years ago. Further, the oldest rock art so far discovered that is age-dated by inference as 8700 years old, is simply a fist-sized rock with scratches on it. To date, no rock art known to be older than about 1000 years resembles the sophistication of design and technique that was used in making these "mammoths."

Although neither of these conjectures is conclusive, the preponderance of evidence so far indicates that the two canyon country "mammoths" are, instead, historic inscriptions depicting modern elephants. Nonetheless, these and other such anomalous rock art creatures have tended to confuse the whole subject of age-dating canyon country rock art. So far, archaeologists have chosen barely to mention such oddities, then ignore them, but sooner or later the problem of extinct or anachronistic animal rock art must be scientifically stated and resolved. The development of a reliable method for the absolute dating of rock art would solve this and many other questions, too, but such a technique is not in sight at present.

ROCK ART STYLES

Earlier paragraphs have noted that some archaeologists use rock art styles to help age-date, classify and otherwise relate rock art to other cultural attributes.

As yet, there is no standard style system for canyon country rock art. The very few archaeologists who have anything to do with this subject have all devised their own systems. In general, these systems divide all canyon country rock art into several overlapping cultural groups, which in turn can be loosely related to our modern time scale by means of the cultural calendar.

Without going into specific style classification systems, or their differences, canyon country rock art can be classified into the following cultural groups:

Archaic: in canyon country this would mean any rock art having pre-Anasazi, pre-Fremont origins. On the time scale, this would be anything older than about 2000 years, or perhaps older than 1500 years in the Fremont region.

Anasazi: this general grouping can be divided further into several sub-groups, largely based upon cultural subdivisions and degrees of cultural development. Anasazi style rock art spans the first 1300 years A.D.

Fremont: which divides into five major sub-groups, one for each of five

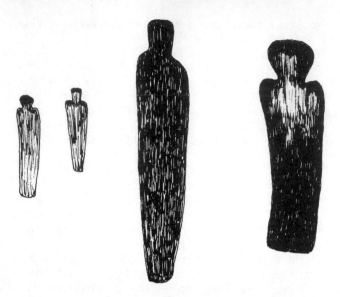

cultural subdivisions, plus, perhaps, a sixth, if the anomalous Horse-shoe Canyon pictographs ultimately turn out to be Fremont. Fremont style rock art spans the period between about 400 and 1350 A.D.

Pre-Anglo contemporary tribes: that is, rock art created by Navajos, Hopis, Utes, Paiutes and others before the arrival of the white man in the mid-1500s. This would include the period from about 1350 to 1550 A.D.

Post-Anglo contemporary tribes: this style is separated from the pre-Anglo mainly because it contains subjects introduced by the Anglo culture, such as horses, hats, guns, trains, etc. This style extends from 1550 A.D. to the present.

Anglo: including Spanish, Mexican and American, from about 1600 A.D. to the present. This style, if the term is appropriate, includes modern vandalism and graffiti.

Some archaeologists would group all post-Anglo rock art—that is, all done by anyone since the Spanish first invaded canyon country in the mid-1500s A.D.—into one "style." Fair arguments can be made in favor of any number of style groupings, but on the whole what matters is that the classification of rock art figures by style of any sort aids in the analysis of the rock art and the related cultures. Rock art "styles" are tools used by archaeologists, and until a style system is universally adopted, each archaeologist will devise and use a system that best suits his needs.

The non-professional who is seriously interested in rock art may find detailed knowledge of rock art styles useful in making tentative identifications of individual figures or panels. The best current sources for such knowledge are the books and reports listed under FURTHER READING and SOURCES that deal exclusively with rock art.

INTERPRETATION

It is difficult to look at a panel of canyon country prehistoric rock art without wondering what it meant, what purpose it served.

Some meanings and purposes seem obvious, such as sympathetic or protective magic, ceremonial, bragging, record-keeping, amusement, story-telling, decorative, religious, artistic and just plain doodling. But with most rock art figures, there is no sure way to tell which is which, and there is a distinct possibility that a particular figure may not fall into any of these categories.

Some prehistoric rock art figures have close or identical equivalents within the art of contemporary Pueblo Indian tribes, and by inference may have the same or similar meanings. Such inferred equivalency is improbable, however, where there is no direct cultural link between past and present. Thus, Navajo designs or figures with known meaning may be similar to Anasazi rock art elements, but this gives no clue as to the Anasazi meaning, because the Navajos are not descendants of the Anasazis. Conversely, meanings for prehistoric Anasazi petroglyphs derived from contemporary Hopi designs have a fair chance of being valid.

One rock art researcher has spent decades developing the concept that rock art is a form of communication, a universal Amerind language of sorts. The weakest link in this concept is, of course, that inferences of meaning taken across cultural lines, or too far into the past, are highly questionable. While it is easy to show that certain figures and symbols have been used by many Amerind cultures over a long period of time, it is not easy to demonstrate that any particular symbol always had the same meaning from tribe to tribe, and from past to present.

It is even more difficult to believe that enough individuals within the stone-age Amerind cultures of canyon country would be able to "read" and "write" such a universal language to make it useful, or to perpetuate it as a standardized communication system. It also pushes the limits of probability to suppose that one tribe or group would care enough about another to bother communicating. Altruism was not a strong point within Stone Age cultures that were perpetually living at the ragged edge of starvation.

In sum, in the eyes of virtually all professional archaeologists, the case for prehistoric rock art's being a form of universal language or communication is still quite weak. Readers who wish to know more about this hypothesis should read Martineau's book, "The Rocks Begin to Speak," listed under FURTHER READING.

For the present, however, most serious students of canyon country rock art are agreed that none of it even approaches the levels of meaning, purpose and sophistication that were reached by the prehistoric cultures of South and Central America and Mexico in their rock carvings and paintings. Canyon country Amerind cultures simply

Intricate Mayan rock carving, Coba ruins, Yucatan Peninsula, Quintana Roo, Mexico.

were not that far advanced, even when the first Europeans reached the western hemisphere and entered canyon country.

LISTING OF ROCK ART SITES

The rock art sites listed in the following section of this book are all within areas presently being given special protection by some agency of state or federal government. Most are within areas administered by the National Park Service, but some are in areas administered by the federal Bureau of Land Management or state agencies. All are protected by some kind of periodic ranger patrol.

Most of the rock art panels at the listed sites are relatively unspoiled by vandalism, but a few are badly defaced. Visitors are admonished not to add to such defacement.

To find the sites listed, consult state and local maps. To locate the rock art within a site, refer to local guide literature. Access modes are noted on the site list and many involve hiking, or an off-road vehicle in some cases.

There are, of course, countless other rock art sites within canyon country, especially within the Fremont territory. Some are listed in books and reports found under FURTHER READING and SOURCES. Others are noted in other guide books in the Canyon Country series, and in the various guide books that describe the region's rivers.

ROCK ART PHOTOGRAPHS

Some of the photographs of rock art, in the pictorial section that follows the listing of sites, depict selected panels or figures at those sites. Others show representative backcountry rock art that may or may not be within the protected areas listed. Where the sites shown are not within such protected areas, only their general locations are given.

All rock art photographs are by the author. None of the petroglyphs or pictographs shown were in any way altered or enhanced before photographing them, although darkroom techniques were used to increase the contrast on some, and a few had already been chalked by someone else. Photographers are advised against such enhancement in the field. Artists and others are warned that any kind of temporary or permanent defacement of rock art violates federal and state laws.

The rock art panels and figures depicted are intended only to be representative. There are far too many sites, or even types of figures, to attempt to show more than a few in a book of this size and general nature.

Some of the books and archaeological reports listed under FURTHER READING and SOURCES have numerous illustrations showing both prehistoric and historic rock art.

Newspaper Rock State Historical Monument, Utah. Note historical petroglyphs showing horseback riders, mixed in with prehistoric images.

207

LISTING OF ROCK ART SITES

STATE	SITE NAME	ROCK ART LOCATIONS AND ACCESS	COMMENTS
ARIZONA	Canyon de Chelly National Monument	See monument literature for locations accessible only by off-road vehicle or guided tour.	Authorized tour guides must accompany private vehicles into Canyon de Chelly.
	Navajo National Monument	See monument literature for locations accessible only by ranger-guided hiking tours.	At times, some sites within the monument may be closed to the public.
	Petrified Forest National Park	See park literature for locations accessible by easy walking.	Some rock art is also on display at the south entrance museum.
COLORADO	Mesa Verde National Park	See park literature for locations accessible by ranger-guided easy walking.	Park also has backcountry sites accessible only by hiking. Contact park rangers for details.
	Colorado National Monument	See monument literature for location in No Thoroughfare Canyon. Accessible by hiking.	Monument also has other rock art in backcountry sites accessible only by hiking. Contact rangers for details.
NEW MEXICO	Bandelier National Monument	See monument literature for locations accessible by easy walking or hiking.	Monument also has backcountry sites accessible only by hiking off established trails. Contact rangers for details.

NEW MEXICO (continued)	Chaco Canyon National Monument	See monument literature for locations accessible by hiking.	Monument also has backcountry sites accessible only by hiking off established trails. Contact rangers for details.
	El Morro National Monument	See monument literature for locations accessible by easy walking.	Monument also has backcountry sites accessible only by hiking off established trails. Contact rangers for details.
	Gila Cliff Dwellings National Monument	See monument literature for locations accessible by hiking.	There are other rock art sites within the surrounding wilderness primitive areas that are accessible only by hiking and backpacking. Contact forest rangers for further information.
	Petroglyph National Monument	Many sites along a cliff face. Easy walking trail to petroglyph panels.	From I-40, take Coors Blvd. to Montano Road to reach visitor center.
UTAH	Arches National Park	See park literature for locations accessible by easy walking.	One location is near the trail to Delicate Arch. Another is above U.S. 191 just north of the Colorado River Bridge.

UTAH (continued)	Canyonlands National Park	See park literature for locations accessible only by hiking or 4x4. See river guide books for locations accessible only by boat.	Principal locations accessible by hiking or ORV are Salt Creek, Horse, Davis, Lavendar and Horseshoe canyons and The Maze. There are numerous other backcountry sites accessible only by backpacking or boating.
	Capitol Reef National Park	See park literature for locations accessible by easy walking or hiking.	Principal locations accessible by walking are beside Utah 24. There are numerous other backcountry sites accessible by hiking or ORV. Contact park rangers for details.
	Zion National Park	See park literature for locations accessible by easy walking or hiking.	Principal locations accessible by walking are within the main canyon. There are many other sites accessible by hiking or ORV. Contact park rangers for details.
	Dinosaur National Monument (Utah and Colorado)	See monument literature for locations accessible by walking or hiking. See river guide books for locations accessible by boat.	Monument has numerous locations in the backcountry accessible only by hiking, boating, or ORV. Contact monument rangers for details.

UTAH (continued)			
	Hovenweep National Monument	See monument literature for locations accessible by easy walking or hiking.	Monument has many backcountry locations accessible only by hiking off of established trails. See monument rangers for details.
	Natural Bridges National Monument	See monument literature for locations accessible by hiking.	Monument has many backcountry locations accessible only by hiking off of established trails. See monument rangers for details.
	Glen Canyon National Recreation Area	See recreation area literature and commercial guide books and maps for locations accessible by boat and hiking.	Much of this region's rock art is now beneath the reservoir waters, but many sites still remain. Some can be reached by boat and hiking, some only by 4x4 or backpacking. Backcountry locations are found only in archaeological reports.
	Newspaper Rock State Historical Monument	Roadside display beside Utah 211, the paved road between U.S. 191 and Canyonlands National Park.	An outstanding display of easily accessible prehistoric and historic rock art. There are other smaller panels within the same stretch of Indian Creek Canyon.

UTAH (continued)	Grand Gulch Primitive Area (BLM)	See primitive area literature for locations accessible by backpacking or guided tour by horseback.	The Grand Gulch canyon system is accessible from three points: Utah 261; Utah 263 and the Collins Spring road; and the San Juan River. Prior registration with BLM rangers is required.
	San Rafael Swell (BLM)	Rock art panels at Temple Mountain Wash and Buckhorn Wash are beside paved or dirt roads accessible to highway vehicles.	The Swell also has many backcountry locations accessible by hiking or 4x4. See Utah Multipurpose Map #2 for road information and locations of Buckhorn and Temple Mountain panels. Backcountry locations are found only in archaeological reports.
	Fremont Indian State Park	Panel is near visitor center.	Park is just off of I-70 and U.S. 89
	Utah Highway 279 (adjacent to BLM land)	Roadside displays beside this paved highway, down the Colorado River gorge, beginning about 4.5 miles from U.S. 191.	Rock art beside Cane Creek Road, on the opposite side of the river, are on private land. Some panels along Utah 279 are above the road level, because talus was removed during construction.

Anasazi petroglyph, Moab Valley, Utah.

Fremont petroglyph of "bowhunter," Ninemile Canyon, Utah.

(Left) Anasazi petroglyph near Batatakin ruin, Navajo National Monument, Arizona.
(Right) Panel detail, Mill Creek Canyon, Utah.

Fremont petroglyphs, Ninemile Canyon, Utah.

One of many petroglyph panels, Colorado River gorge, beside Utah 279.

Panel detail, Colorado River gorge, beside Utah 279. Note that the figures are carrying "shields" and wearing large ear pendants.

Historic petroglyph, Montezuma Canyon, Utah.

Geometric pattern petroglyph, Petrified Forest National Park, Arizona, Anasazi culture.

One of many Fremont petroglyph panels in Ninemile Canyon, Utah. Note damage to the panel from scaling rock.

Part of the Thirteen Faces pictograph panel, Horse Creek Canyon, Canyonlands National Park, Utah.

217

Four Faces pictographs, upper Salt Creek Canyon, Canyonlands National Park, probably Anasazi.

Petroglyph panel, Colorado River gorge, beside Utah 279. Note the white substance left by someone trying to reproduce the 'glyphs. Such techniques are illegal. Photography is the best way to reproduce rock art without risking damage to it.

Anasazi petroglyph of a cougar, Petrified Forest National Park, Arizona.

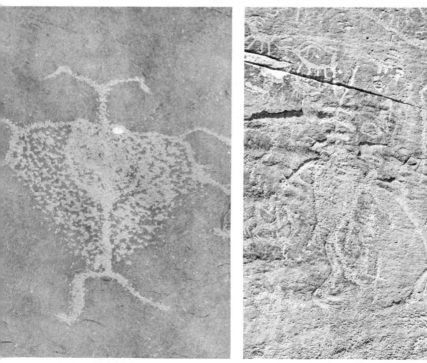

(Left) Moab Valley, Utah. (Right) Detail from a large Anasazi petroglyph panel, San Juan River gorge at Sand Island, in Utah.

Ninemile Canyon, Utah.

Detail from large Anasazi petroglyph panel, San Juan River gorge, Utah.

Detail of a large pictograph panel, Arches National Park, Utah, probably Fremont.

A Kokopelli flute-player, San Juan River gorge, Utah. The figure on the right appears to be attacking Kokopelli.

One of Thirteen Faces, Horse Canyon, Canyonlands National Park, Utah.

"Horned rattlesnake" pictograph, Buckhorn Wash, San Rafael Well, Utah, outlined with chalk by someone, and vandalized with a bullet hole.

Pictograph panel in Horseshoe Canyon Annex, Canyonlands National Park, Utah.

Pictograph panel above small granary, upper Salt Creek Canyon, Canyonlands National Park, Utah.

Anasazi petroglyph, Indian Creek Canyon, Utah.

Snake petroglyph, Sego Canyon, Utah.

Fremont petroglyphs, Ninemile Canyon, Utah. Note historic inscription beside the 'glyphs.

(Left) Faded "negative" pictograph, near Betatakin ruin, Navajo National Monument, Arizona. (Right) Anasazi petroglyph, San Juan River gorge, Utah.

(Left) Anasazi petroglyph, Petrified Forest National Park, Arizona. (Right) Detail from one petroglyph panel, Behind-the-Rocks, Utah. Note the two "fighting" figures on the left.

Anasazi petroglyphs near Una Vida ruin, Chaco Canyon National Monument, New Mexico.

Curious box-bodied desert sheep, Sevenmile Canyon, Utah. Note tiny figure of lamb below central figure.

Pictograph panel in an alcove, Black Dragon Canyon, San Rafael Swell, Utah. Note apparent record-keeping or counting. Probably Fremont culture.

Five Faces pictograph, Davis Canyon, Canyonlands National Park, Utah, probably Anasazi. The faces are at a ceremonial site far from any dwellings.

Petroglyph panel, Petrified Forest National Park, Arizona.

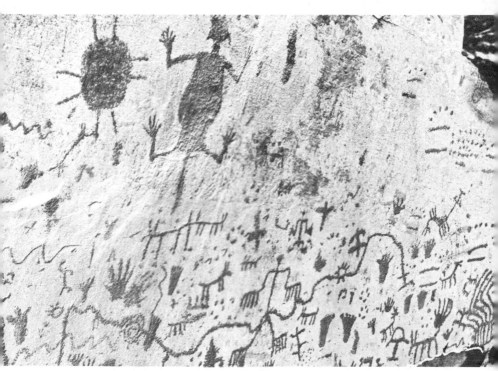

Negative print of the same panel, illustrating a photographic technique for increasing 'glyph contrast for study.

Anasazi petroglyph panel, Cane Creek Canyon, Utah.

(Left) Behind-the-Rocks, Utah. (Right) Anasazi petroglyphs, Petrified Forest National Park, Arizona.

*Historic petroglyphs, **Salt Wash**, Arches National Park, Utah. Note the four horseback riders.*

"Mammoth" petroglyph, Indian Creek Canyon, Utah. This 'glyph was probably done by historic Indians who had seen an elephant. For scale, note 25c coin in lower left.

Badly vandalized Fremont pictographs, Buckhorn Wash, San Rafael Swell, Utah.

Fremont petroglyph, Ninemile Canyon, Utah. Note the several bullet holes.

"Fighting" figures, Behind-the-Rocks, Utah.

Detail from the largest pictograph panel, Horseshoe Canyon Annex, Canyonlands National Park, Utah.

(Left) Fremont pictographs, Black Dragon Canyon, San Rafael Swell, Utah. Note that someone has vandalized one figure with bullets, the other by changing its face, and both by chalking them. (Right) Two-headed petroglyph figure, Indian Creek Canyon, Utah.

234

Petroglyphs in the San Juan River gorge, Utah, culture unknown.

Anasazi pictographs, upper Salt Creek Canyon, Canyonlands National Park, Utah.

235

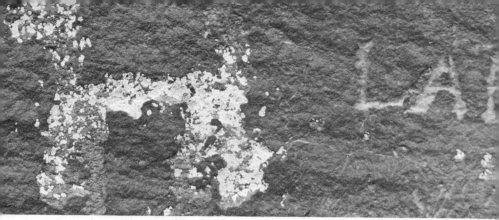

Small Fremont petroglyph, Ninemile Canyon, Utah. Note that lichens are growing in the 'glyph, but not in the more recent scribings.

San Juan River gorge, Utah. Note that someone has partially "renewed" the right-hand figure by chipping at the desert varnish that had formed within the figure.

Detail from a large petroglyph panel, Moab Valley, Utah.

(Left) Fremont desert sheep, Fremont River gorge, Capitol Reef National Park, Utah. (Right) San Juan River gorge, Utah. Note small human figure within head of large 'glyph.

(Left) Detail of Fremont petroglyph panel, Sego Canyon, Utah. (Right) One of many Anasazi petroglyph panels in Valley of Fire State Park, Nevada.

"Santa's sleigh and reindeer," Moab Valley, Utah. Despite its novelty, the panel has been vandalized.

Row of painted spots and "turtle" figures, Salt Creek Canyon, Canyonlands National Park, Utah.

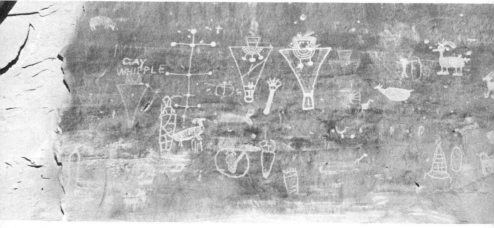

Fremont petroglyphs, Sego Canyon, Utah.

238

Row of humpbacked figures led by flute-playing Kokopelli, Behind-the-Rocks, Utah.

"Supernatural" image, Ninemile Canyon, Utah. Note smaller "supplicating" human figure on the right.

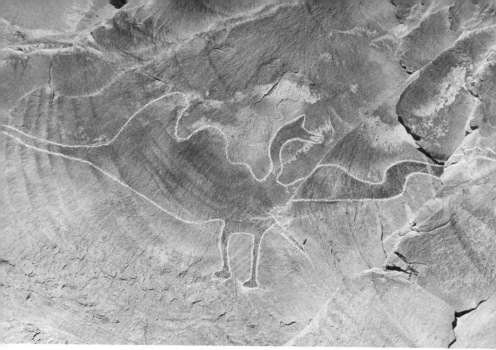

Dragon-like pictograph in Black Dragon Canyon, San Rafael Swell, Utah. Chalk outline has been added by someone to accent the faded outline of the reddish figure.

(Left) Anasazi petroglyph, San Juan River gorge, Utah. (Right) Indian Creek Canyon, Utah.

(Lett) Petroglyph sandal prints, Arches National Park, Utah. (Right) Petroglyph, Colorado River gorge, near Moab, Utah. Note necklace on human figure.

(Left) Detail from a larger panel, Colorado River gorge, beside Utah 279. (Right) Anasazi pictograph, Horse Canyon, Canyonlands National Park, Utah. Image is one of "Thirteen Faces."

241

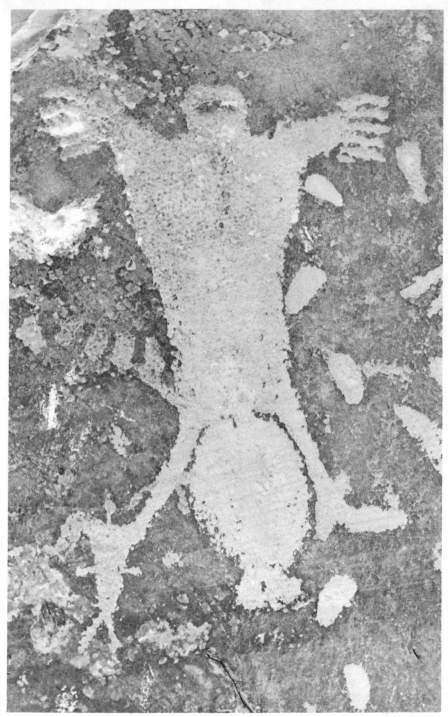

Detail from petroglyph panel, Cane Creek Canyon, Utah. Figure is apparently a woman giving birth.

Detail from largest pictograph panel, Horseshoe Canyon Annex, Canyonlands National Park, Utah, culture uncertain.

Historic petroglyphs, Fremont River gorge, Capitol Reef National Park, Utah.

Newspaper Rock State Historical Monument, Utah. Note historic petroglyphs of horseback riders among the prehistoric 'glyphs.

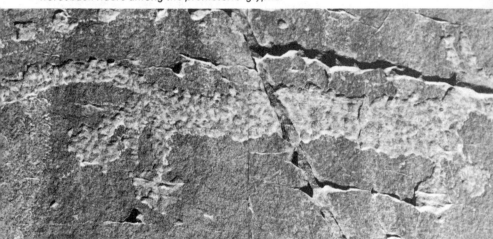

Animal figure, probably cougar, in Sevenmile Canyon, Utah.

Detail from large Anasazı petroglyph panel, San Juan River gorge, Utah.

244

Detail of large pictograph panel, Horseshoe Canyon Annex, Canyonlands National Park, Utah, culture uncertain.

Mill Creek Canyon, near Moab, Utah.

Fremont petroglyphs, Fremont River gorge, Capitol Reef National Park, Utah. Note the numerous bullet holes in the two larger figures.

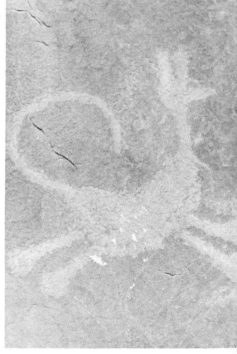

(Left) Chalked pictographs, Black Dragon Canyon, San Rafael Swell, Utah, probably Fremont. (Right) Small petroglyph, Moab Valley, Utah, probably Anasazi.

246

LITERATURE

Further Reading
Sources
Textbooks
Rock Art
Site Studies
General

White House ruins, Canyon de Chelly National Monument, Arizona.

FURTHER READING

The books listed below were all written for readers with average backgrounds in natural and human history, and thus make easy and rewarding reading for almost anyone. Some of the books listed are not exclusively about the prehistoric Indian cultures of the general Four Corners region, but nonetheless contain enough such information to make them well worth reading by those interested in this subject. For further reading of a more technical nature, refer to the literature listed under SOURCES.

Dictionary of Prehistoric Indian Artifacts of the American Southwest, Barnett, Northland Press.
Prehistoric Mesoamerica, Adams, Little, Brown & Co.
Man's Rise to Civilization, Farb, Dutton.
Standing Up Country, The Canyon Lands of Utah and Arizona, Crampton, Knopf.
Beginner's Guide to Archaeology, Brennan, Stackpole.
The Archaeology of North America, Snow & Forman, Viking Press.
The First Americans, Claiborne, Time-Life.
Archaeology and Archaeological Resources, Society for American Archaeology (booklet).
Indians, Brandon, American Heritage.
Anasazi, Pike & Muench, American West.
1000 Million Years on the Colorado Plateau, Look, Bell Publications.
The Trail of the Ancients, Lyman, Trail of the Ancients Association.
The Story of Inscription Rock, Dodge, Phoenix Publishing.
The Exploration of the Colorado River and its Canyons, Powell, Dover
The Romance of the Colorado River, Dellenbaugh, Rio Grande.
Coronado on the Turquoise Trail, Bolton, University of New Mexico Press.
Pageant in the Wilderness, Bolton, Utah State Historical Society.
Mesa Verde & Rocky Mountain National Parks, Breternitz & Smith, World-Wide Research & Publishing.
Wind in the Rock, Zwinger, Harper & Row.
Run, River, Run, Zwinger, Harper & Row.
The Rocks Begin to Speak, Martineau, K C Publications.
Canyon Graphics and Graffiti, Utah Museum of Natural History.
The Cliff Dwellers of the Mesa Verde, Nordenskiold, Rio Grande Press.
Prehistoric Petroglyphs and Pictographs in Utah, Siegrist, Utah Museum of Fine Arts.
The Archaeology of Arizona, Martin & Plog, Doubleday.
Prehistoric Southwestern Craft Arts, Tanner, University of Arizona Press.
Prehistory of the Far West, Cressman, University of Utah Press.

Southwestern Indian Tribes, Bahti, K C Publications.

The World of the American Indian, National Geographic.

Canyon de Chelly, Its People and Rock Art, Grant, University of Arizona Press.

River Runner's Guide to Dinosaur National Monument & Vicinity, Hayes & Simmons, Powell Society.

River Runner's Guide to Canyonlands National Park & Vicinity, Mutschler, Powell Society.

River Runner's Guide to the Canyons of the Green & Colorado Rivers—Labyrinth, Stillwater & Cataract Canyons, Mutschler, Powell Society.

River Runner's Guide to the Canyons of the Green & Colorado Rivers—Desolation & Gray Canyons, Mutschler, Powell Soceity.

Geology of the Canyons of the San Juan River, Baars, Four Corners Geological Society.

Desolation River Guide, Evans & Belknap, Westwater Books.

Dinosaur River Guide, Evans & Belknap, Westwater Books.

Grand Canyon River Guide, Belknap, Westwater Books.

Canyonlands River Guide, Belknap & Belknap, Westwater Books.

Guidebook to the Colorado River, Moab to Hite, Rigby, Hamblin, Matheny & Welsh, Department of Geology, Brigham Young University.

Canyon Country Paddles, Huser, Wasatch Publishers.

SOURCES

Following is a partial list of literature sources used by the authors in the preparation of this book. Almost all of the titles listed are textbooks or scientific papers, some of these book-sized, that were written by professional archaeologists for other archaeologists. They thus do not make easy reading for the average person.

They are, however, rich sources of detailed information for those who are willing and able to tolerate and understand the stylized format and prose of the archaeological profession. Most are heavily illustrated with photographs, sketches, charts and maps, and may be of value to the casual reader for this, if nothing else.

TEXTBOOKS

Jennings, *Prehistory of North America*, McGraw-Hill, 1974.
Spencer & Jennings, *The Native Americans*, Harper & Row, 1965.

ROCK ART

Aikens, C. Melvin, *Indian Petroglyphs from White Pine County, Nevada*, Anthropological Paper No. 99, Miscellaneous Collected Papers 19-24, Paper No. 19, University of Utah Press, 1978.
Busby, C. Fleming, R., Hayes, R. & Nissen, K., *The Manufacture of Petroglyphs: Additional Replicative Experiments from the Western Great Basin*, North American Rock Art, No. 1, Ballena Press Publications, Socorro, New Mexico, 1978.
Castleton, Kenneth B., M.D., *Petroglyphs and Pictographs of Utah, Volume One: The East and Northeast*, Utah Museum of Natural History, 1978.
Garvin, Gloria, *Shamans and Rock Art Symbols*, North American Rock Art, No. 1, Ballena Press Publications, Socorro, New Mexico, 1978.
Gibson, Robert & Singer, Clay, *Ven-195: Treasure House of Prehistoric Cave Art*, North American Rock Art, No. 1, Ballena Press Publications, Socorro, New Mexico, 1978.
Heizer, Robert F. & Hester, Thomas R., *Two Petroglyph Sites in Lincoln County, Nevada*, North American Rock Art, No. 1, Ballena Press Publications, Socorro, New Mexico 1978.
Schaafsma, Polly, *The Rock Art of Utah*, Papers of the Peabody Museum of Archaeology and Ethnology, Harvard University, Vol. 65, Cambridge, 1971.
Schaafsma, Polly, *The Rock Art of New Mexico*, Cultural Properties Review Committee, University of New Mexico Press, Albuquerque, 1975.

Schaafsma, Polly, *A Survey of Tsegi Canyon Rock Art*, National Park Service, unpublished.

Swartz, Jr., B.K., *Aluminum Powder: A Technique for Photographically Recording Petroglyphs*, American Antiquity, Vol. 28, No. 3, pp. 400-401, 1963.

Turner II, Christy G., *Petrographs of the Glen Canyon Region*, Glen Canyon Series No. 4, Museum of Northern Arizona Bulletin No. 38, 1963.

Wellmann, Klaus F., *Kokopelli of Indian Paleology*, Journal of the American Medical Association, Volume 212, June 8, 1970.

SITE STUDIES

Agenbroad, Larry D., *The Alluvial Geology of Upper Grand Gulch, Utah; its Relationship to Anasazi Inhabitation of the Cedar Mesa Area*, A Guidebook of the Four Corners Geological Society, Eighth Field Conference, 1975.

Aikens, C. Melvin, *Hogup Cave*, Anthropological Paper No. 93, University of Utah Press, 1970.

Anderson, Keith M., *Archaeology on the Shonto Plateau, Northeast Arizona*, Southwestern Monuments Association, Technical Series, Volume 7, 1969.

Bannister, Bryant, *Tree-Ring Dating of the Archaeological Sites in the Chaco Canyon Region, New Mexico*, Southwest Parks and Monuments, Technical Series, Volume 6, Part 2, 1964.

Berry, Michael S., *An Archaeological Survey of the Northeast Portion of Arches National Monument*, Antiquities Section Selected Papers, Vol. 1, No. 1-3, Utah State Historical Society, 1975.

Day, Kent C. & Dibble, David S., *Archaeological Survey of the Flaming Gorge Reservoir Area, Wyoming-Utah*, Anthropological Paper No. 65, Department of Anthropology, University of Utah, 1963.

Fowler, Don D., *1961 Excavations, Harris Wash, Utah*, Anthropological Paper No. 64, Department of Anthropology, University of Utah, 1963.

Fowler, Don D. & Aikens, C. Melvin, *1961 Excavations, Kaiparowits Plateau, Utah*, Anthropological Paper No. 66, Department of Anthropology, University of Utah, 1963.

Fowler, Don D. & Matley, John F., *The Palmer Collection from Southwestern Utah, 1875*, Anthropological Paper No. 99, Miscellaneous Collected Papers 19-24, Paper No. 20, University of Utah Press, 1978.

Fry, Gary F., *Prehistoric Diet at Danger Cave, Utah, as Determined by the Analysis of Coprolites*, Anthropological Paper No. 99, Miscellaneous Collected Papers 19-24, Paper No. 23, University of Utah Press, 1978.

Gillin, John, *Archaeological Investigations in Nine Mile Canyon, Utah: A Re-publication*, Anthropological Paper No. 21, Department of Anthropology, University of Utah, 1955.

deHaan, Petrus A., *An Archaeological Survey of Lower Montezuma Canyon, Southeastern Utah*, Department of Anthropology and Archaeology, Brigham Young University, 1972, unpublished.

Hartman, Dana, *Tuzigoot, An Archaeological Overview*, Museum of Northern Arizona Research Paper No. 4, 1976.

Hartman, Dana, & Wolf, Arthur H., *Wupatki, an Archaeological Assessment*, Museum of Northern Arizona Research Paper No. 6, 1977.

Hobler, Philip M. & Hobler, Audrey E., *An Archaeological Survey of the Upper White Canyon Area, Southeastern Utah*, Antiquities Section Selected Papers, Vol. 5, No. 13, Utah State Historical Society, 1978.

Hunt, Alice P. & Wilson, Bates, *Archaeological Sites in the Horse Canyon Area, San Juan County, Utah*, National Park Service 1952, unpublished.

Jennings, Jesse D., *Danger Cave*, Anthropological Papers No. 27, Department of Anthropology, University of Utah, 1957.

Lipe, William D., & Breed, William J., & West, James, *Lake Pagahrit, Southeastern Utah—A Preliminary Research Report*, A Guidebook of the Four Corners Geological Society, Eighth Field Conference, 1975.

Lipe, William D. & Matson, R. G., *Archeology and Alluvium in the Grand Gulch—Cedar Mesa Area, Southeastern Utah*, A Guidebook of the Four Corners Geological Society, Eighth Field Conference, 1975.

Long, Jr., Paul V., *Archeological Excavations in Lower Glen Canyon, Utah, 1959-60*, Glen Canyon Series No. 7, Museum of Northern Arizona Bulletin No. 42, 1966.

Madsen, David B., *Three Fremont Sites in Emery County, Utah*, Antiquities Section Selected Papers, Vol 1, No. 1-3, Utah State Historical Society, 1975.

Marwitt, John P., *Median Village and Fremont Regional Variation*, Anthropological Papers No. 95, University of Utah Press, 1970.

Miller, Donald, E., *A Synthesis of Excavations at Site 42SA863, Three Kiva Pueblo, Montezuma Canyon, San Juan County, Utah*, Department of Anthropology and Archeology, Brigham Young University, 1974, unpublished.

Patterson, Gregory R., *A Preliminary Study of an Anasazi Settlement (42SA971) Prior to A.D. 900 in Montezuma Canyon, San Juan County, Southeastern Utah*, Department of Anthropology and Archeology, Brigham Young Univeristy, 1975, unpublished.

Richert, Roland, *Excavation of a Portion of the East Ruins, Aztec Ruins National Monument, New Mexico*, Southwest Monuments Association, Technical Series, Volume 4, 1964.

Sharrock, F.W., *An Archeological Survey of Canyonlands National Park*, Department of Anthropology, University of Utah, 1966.

Schroedl, Alan R. & Hogan, Patrick F., *Innocents Ridge and the San Rafael Fremont*, Antiquities Section Selected Papers, Vol. 1, No. 1-3, Utah State Historical Society, 1975.

Schwartz, Douglas W., *Grand Canyon Prehistory*, Geology and Natural History of the Fifth Field Conference, Powell Centennial River Expedition, Four Corners Geological Society, 1969.

Shutler, Jr., Richard, & Shutler, Mary Elizabeth, *Archeological Survey in Southern Nevada*, Nevada State Museum, Anthropological Paper No. 7, 1962.

Shields, Wayne F., *The Woodruff Bison Kill*, Anthropological Paper No. 99, Miscellaneous Collected Papers 19-24, Paper No. 21, University of Utah Press, 1978.

Shields, Wayne F., & Dalley, Gardiner F., *The Bear River No. 3 Site*, Anthropological Paper No. 99, Miscellaneous Collected Papers 19-24, Paper No. 21, University of Utah Press, 1978.

Vivian, Gordon, & Mathews, Tom W., *Kin Kletso, a Pueblo III Community in Chaco Canyon, New Mexico*, Southwest Parks and Monuments, Technical Series, Volume 6, Part 1, 1964.

Ward, Albert E., *Inscription House*, Museum of Northern Arizona Technical Series No. 16, 1975.

GENERAL

Ambler, J. Richard, *The Anasazi*, Museum of Northern Arizona, 1977.

Chavez, Fray Angelico (translator), *The Dominguez-Escalante Journal*, Brigham Young University Press, 1976.

Dean, Jeffrey S., *Tree-Ring Dating in Archaeology*, Anthropological Paper No. 99, Miscellaneous Collected Papers 19-24, Paper No. 24, University of Utah Press, 1978.

Gunnerson, James H., *The Fremont Culture: A Study in Cultural Dynamics on the Northern Anasazi Frontier*, Papers of the Peabody Museum of Archaeology and Ethnology, Harvard University, Volume 59, No. 2, The Peabody Museum, Cambridge, 1969.

Jennings, Jesse D., *Glen Canyon, A Summary*, Anthropological Papers No. 81, Department of Anthropology, University of Utah, 1966.

Jennings, Jesse D., *Prehistory of Utah and the Eastern Great Basin*, Anthropological Paper No. 98, University of Utah Press, 1978.

Morss, Noel, *The Ancient Culture of the Fremont River in Utah, Report on the Explorations under the Claflin-Emerson Fund, 1928-29*, Papers of the Peabody Museum of American Archaeology Ethnology, Harvard University, 1931, reprint Kraus Reprint Co., 1978.

Newberry, J.S., *Report of the Exploring Expedition from Santa Fe, New Mexico, to the Junction of the Grand and Green Rivers of the Great Colorado of the West, in 1859*, under command of Captain J. N. Macomb, Corps of Topographical Engineers, U.S. Army, U.S. Government Printing Office, 1876.

Pattison, N.B., & Potter, L.D., *Prehistoric and Historic Steps and Trails of Glen Canyon-Lake Powell*, Lake Powell Research Project Bulletin No. 45, National Science Foundation, 1977.

Steward, Julian H., *Basin-Plateau Aboriginal Sociopolitical Groups*, Smithsonian Institution Bureau of American Ethnology, Bulletin No. 120, U.S. Government Printing Office, 1938, reprint University of Utah Press, 1970.

Wormington, H.M., *Prehistoric Indians of the Southwest*, Denver Museum of Natural History, Denver, 1947.

Site Etiquette

Archeological sites are being damaged by increasing visitation. Many seemingly insignificant impacts, when multiplied by the increasing number of visitors, are causing significant destruction of the clues used by archaeologists to learn about the past. These sites are fragile and irreplaceable, so please be careful when visiting a site and follow these guidelines.

1.   As you approach an archaeological site, stop for a moment and think about how you can minimize your impact.

2.   Stay off the midden (Usually a low mound near the site which is the trash pile left by the original inhabitants.), especially in alcove sites where the midden may have a steep, easily eroded side.

3.   Walls that are stressed once too often can suddenly collapse. Please don't use them as handholds to gain access to a site and don't stand or climb on them.

4.   Please stay on the trail and avoid walking along the base of walls built on slopes. Erosion on the base of walls causes them to topple.

5.   If you pick up an artifact (including prehistoric corn cobs), please replace it where you found it. Moving artifacts from one portion of a site to another makes it difficult to chart a site's growth. Removing artifacts is illegal.

6.   Charcoal and soot are used to date sites. Modern charcoal and soot contaminate the record, so please don't build fires or camp within a site.

7.   Now technology makes it possible to date rock art by analyzing the patina that has built up over the millennia. This patina can be altered by touching it or enhancing it for photography through scratching, pecking, chalking, or oiling. Please refrain from touching it or from using any enhancement techniques.

8.   Children's natural curiosity and enthusiasm for climbing is easily aroused by the walls, nooks, and crannies found at many archaeological sites. Please hold their hands while visiting a site.

Courtesy Rick Moore
Grand Canyon Trust

CANYON COUNTRY BOOKS AND MAPS

-- UTAH CANYON COUNTRY
1. *Canyon Country* HIGHWAY TOURING   (out of print)
2. *Canyon Country* EXPLORING
3. *Canyon Country* HIKING
4. *Canyon Country* ISLAND AREA, Off-Road Vehicle Trails
5. *Canyon Country* ISLAND AREA, Off-Road Vehicle Trail Map
6. *Canyon Country* ARCHES & LA SALS AREA, Off-Road Vehicle Trails
7. *Canyon Country* ARCHES & LA SALS AREA, Off-Road Vehicle Trail Map
8. *Canyon Country* CANYON RIMS & NEEDLES AREAS, Off-Road Vehicle Trails
9. *Canyon Country* CANYON RIMS & NEEDLES AREAS, Off-Road Vehicle Trail Map
10. *Canyon Country* CAMPING
11. *Canyon Country* GEOLOGY
12. *Canyon Country* PADDLES   (out of print)
13. *Canyon Country* PREHISTORIC INDIANS
14. *Canyon Country* PREHISTORIC ROCK ART
15. *Canyon Country* ARCHES & BRIDGES
16. CANYONLANDS NATIONAL PARK, Early History & First Descriptions
17. *Canyon Country* MOUNTAIN BIKING
18. *Canyon Country* MAZE AREA, Off-Road Vehicle Trails
19. *Canyon Country* MAZE AREA, Off-Road Vehicle Trail Map
20. HIKING THE HISTORIC ROUTE of the 1859 MACOMB EXPEDITION
21. *Canyon Country* SLICKROCK HIKING & BIKING
22. *Canyon Country's* KOKOPELLI'S TRAIL -- (Mountain Bike Trail System, Moab to Loma)
23. *Canyon Country's* CANYON RIMS RECREATION AREA
24. *Canyon Country* CANYON RIMS RECREATION AREA, Off-Road Vehicle Trail Map
25. *Canyon Country* CANYON RIMS RECREATION AREA, Off-Road Vehicle Trails
26. *Canyon Country* MOAB AREA MAP
27. MOUNTAIN BIKING in CANYON RIMS RECREATION AREA
28. CAMEO CLIFFS -- Hiking - Biking - Four-Wheeling (public land recreation area)
29. Map of CAMEO CLIFFS (public land recreation area)
30. GEOLOGY of the MOAB AREA
31. REISEN AUF DEN HIGHWAYS IM CANYON COUNTRY (German language version of #1 book
32. *Canyon Country's* Canyon Rims Recreation Area MOUNTAIN BIKE CHALLENGE ROUTE MA
33. *Canyon Country* EXPLORER #1
34. *Canyon Country's* LA SAL MOUNTAINS - Hiking & Nature Handbook
35. Map of Moab's SLICKROCK BIKE TRAIL & SAND FLATS RECREATION AREA
36. Map of KOKOPELLI'S BIKE TRAIL -- (Mountain Bike Trail System, Moab to Loma)
37. Recreation Map of the SAN RAFAEL SWELL & SAN RAFAEL DESERT
38. GEOLOGY of CANYON COUNTRY (chart based on #30 book)
39. HIKER'S & SKIER'S MAP of the LA SAL MOUNTAINS
40. *Canyon Country* EXPLORER #2
41. Recreation Map of the ABAJO MOUNTAINS & ELK RIDGE AREA
42. Hiking in the SAND FLATS RECREATION AREA

These books and maps can be purchased from retail outlets throughout Utah and are available by mail from Wasatch Publishers. Send for a free catalog.

Wasatch Publishers 4460 Ashford Drive, Salt Lake City, UT 84124

Trade distribution by:
Wasatch Book Distribution, P.O. Box 1108 Salt Lake City, Utah, 84110
Trade distribution in Southeast Utah by:
Canyon Country Publications, P.O. Box 963, Moab, Utah, 84532